A VIBRANT AWAKENING OF MEMORIES

Happy Birthday
Beautiful ♡
xoxo - Kathy
2023

A VIBRANT AWAKENING OF MEMORIES

Progressive Home Health's First Edition of Poetry Workshop Poems

JOHN CONTE

PITTSBURGH AREA LONG TERM CARE RESIDENTS

EMILY MORRIS

ISBN-13: 9781547193011
ISBN-10: 1547193018

FRANCISCAN MANOR

"Still Me"

Looking at my photograph
I know I can be anybody
But with memories
I see my past like a movie...

I recall the leaves in the fall
The smell of barbecue on the grill
The sound of water falls and rain
The taste of crispy turkey skin
Holding hands at the Thanksgiving table
I see my eyes and they are still the same
With my memories I'm "Still Me."
I recall burning leaves in the fall
The smell of barbecue on the grill
The sound of water falls and rain
The taste of crispy turkey skin
Holding hands at the table at Thanksgiving
I see my eyes and they're the same
With my memories I'm "Still Me"
I recall burning leaves in the fall
The smell of barbecue on the grill
The sound of water falls and rain
The taste of crispy turkey skin
Holding hands at the table at Thanksgiving
I see my eyes and they're the same
With my memories I'm "Still Me"
Written for Franciscan Manor
November 15, 2016
By Progressive Home Health's
Resident Poet John Conte

CHAPTER 1

JANUARY/FEBRUARY

Country Meadows

Pittsburgh is who we are
Clay from the picturesque hills to baked bricks for roads and coal from
valleys shipped to Pittsburgh to make steel; iron and ore; filled barges
passing under bridges along 3 rivers; tunnels and taverns – are all part of
an American epic created here in our metropolitan Pittsburgh. We have
reminders of other things forged here too, like independence. Freedom
is not only a town George Washington slept in as a commander; the
"underground railroad" freed many men, women, and children to come.
Pittsburgh is who we are and with a strong sense of community never far.

Pretty City
No longer veiled in a cloud of smoke.
Now unveiled in healing of the three rivers' sands.-
blown clean with heated air to create glass-stained brilliant
colors of butterflies and peonies.
All through walks in North and Olympia Parks.
Mt. Washington vista—sun sparkling PPG Place.
Bedazzling jewels of geometry frozen like a lake.
Pretty city with a rainbow even if the Steelers lost.
For Pittsburgher's find hope, if and within, at all costs.
Written By: The Residents of Country Meadows, South Hills
Date: February 5, 2016

Independence Court

Girl by the River with Skinny Legs

Ice box on the porch filled with milk and ice delivered
even before we started walking to school in the morning.
Bells ringing!
And often times a head or two a day... pranks and sometimes
mean jokes aimed and played. Nope! You didn't bring us down
to your stunted class. The poets in the room are now kings and
queens, you see.

Thought of the Day (in Pittsburgh)

Melting pot! There it is. The truth be told.
All different, yet we all bleed "Black & Gold" Yeah,
around here, we speak our own language. Outsiders are
sometimes taken-a-back by this! But still they get that
we're a friendly kinda city.
Pretty gritty. Clapping erasers. Chalkboard's ready! Out of
nothing. We are something. Heinz 57 bold!
Written By: The Residents of Independence Court, Monroeville
Date: February 11, 2016

North Hills Health and Rehab

Our Generation Has Seen So Many Changes
I've found a friend in the weather.
And found the reasons the seasons always
create such profound memories for me.
A rainy day downtown for work definitely feels this way -
and certain days with the seasons always bring a change.
Rail trolleys cut through dirty coal dust passing by phone
booths on squirted off concrete sidewalks and street lamps
being lit during extraordinary times of extreme air pollution.
So, when we are asked, "Do you like the new things or do
you think you would rather live in the past?" Think Spring!
Fragrant colorful blossoms and soft blouses without coal dust.
We like our air fresh nowadays just like a walk in North Park.

A Story Untold That Tells Who We Are
Women did not only do the canning of fruit and vegetables.
We weren't always indoors in the kitchens and in the cellars.
We were also found on pitching mounds and playing in outfields.
Throwing fast balls and hitting far so we could round the bases.
We often found ourselves running so hard in schoolyard races.
Oh how my brother cried telling how he lost to a girl at the table.
There we were playing checkers and I "double-jumped" him to win.
Written By: The Residents of North Hills Health and Rehab
Date: February 15, 2016

Rochester Manor and Villa

A Pearl Necklace on Smithfield Street

I recall wintertime city shoppers during Christmas season smiling like stars.

Strings of lights with pretty white, perfectly round bulbs glowing with electricity.

Up on Mt. Washington and peering down at the sparkling city brilliant at night.

Top of the Smithfield Street Bridge looks like an elegant Mabe pearl necklace.

White roses. Pretty red roses. It was St. Valentine's Day last weekend before.

It was flowers galore here as if a rainbow fell down to earth for the time being.

But, yes, spring is a good time indeed - come late February snow, come flowers.

Written By: The Residents of Rochester Manor and Villa

Date: February 17, 2016

Willow Lane

We Grew Everything

Everything! Cabbage, corn, tomatoes, parsley
and all the other herbs! Parsnips, turnips, carrots,
beets grown underground. The root vegetables.
And with the roots from the sassafras trees -
we dug'em-up and we made a very tasty tea
Elderberry jelly. Well, despite the prohibition,
we even made elderberry wine and our own beer too!
Growing everything on our farms around Pittsburgh.

I Learned a Lot Today

Her brother was a welder at Dravo Corporation.
It was a family environment with picnics and
they had swimming pools for the kids and everybody.
Women worked in the cafeteria and in the printing department.
Men built big LST's on Neville Island that floated from the Ohio River
reaching the mighty Mississippi River all the way to the Gulf of Mexico.
When we weren't at school with our friends, working, or picnicking with family.
we had our heads in both of our hands listening to the radio until Mazeroski
hit a huge home run and the Pittsburgh Pirates won the World Series, man!
It was 1960 and all the women ran into the streets screaming, - me too, pregnant.
Written By: The Residents of Willow Lane
Date: February 18, 2016

ManorCare

Fiery Red Roses on Stems
I can remember the smell...
Making steel smells a lot like rotten eggs —
Even though the colors look like pretty roses
Velvety, thick hot molten peach colored roses.
Red as the hot metals and yellow hot as fire
Steel mills have nice bright colors but not smells!
Reminds me of a similar situation in Green Tree, PA
Kids playing and pretty bushes cutting the skin of limbs
Blood red from sturdy pricks along the stem of roses

Home Made
Ready to can garden fruit and vegetables for winter,
They also bought a whole cow and canned that too!
And, that Tom Friday's place along California Avenue --
The place with a red awning, he still cuts his own meat.
People used to can butchered beef meat and the produce.
I canned apple butter. Yep, we all had homemade stuff...
Wine, root beer, pickles, sauerkraut, boysen and elder berry jelly.
And we had uses for this stuff, not just to eat but for medicine.
Homemade boiled onions in sugar water with honey and lemon,
Our cough syrup! And muslin mustard plaster on top of your chest.
Written By: The Residents of ManorCare, GreenTree
Date: February 23, 2016

North Hills Health and Rehab

Great St. Patrick's Day Flood of 1936

Winter in 1936, January and February blanketed Pittsburgh with snow
A welcomed warm snap mid-March brought what many did not know...
What would happen next? All Three Rivers with melting snow and ice did flow
March 17th found Pittsburgh experiencing a St. Patrick's Day flood...
25 feet and yet to crest and that night brought heavy rain from big storms
The pounding rain made the snow and ice melt even faster and by midnight
Flood waters had risen to over 34 feet moving from The Point to downtown
Wednesday afternoon of March 18th, the river levels peaked at 46 feet...
With no electricity people used oil lamps and Coleman lanterns to carry on
River rescues had to take place with all buildings flooded up 3 to 4 stories
March 19th the water receded a bit but not much until like it did March 21st
City people had to navigate themselves in boats using coal shovels as oars
And then the aftermath of murky flood mess even contaminating good water
Everything had to be cleaned up, sterilized, and fixed up, even the giant mills
For days, flood water took over Pittsburgh including machinery of steel wheels
It would not be for some good years later a system of dams built for control
Lives lost. Business ruined. Yet the fabric of Pittsburgh was still a city in total.
Written By: The Residents of North Hills Health and Rehab
Date: March 7, 2016

North Hills Health and Rehab

Community

At North Park, we use to picnic by where we skated on the frozen pond
In the spring, summer, and fall, our sense of community was set so strong
Company, school, and church picnics and family reunion picnics all day long!
The Alice Chalmers company picnic paid for everything for your family...
You could win a car at St. Michael's on the South Side's Carson Street!!
My brother won a race at West View Park's August annual. Wasn't beaten!
Back then women and girls would buy at Pittsburgh Mercantile, South Side
J&L Steel mills lighting up the sky with a huge fiery glow against the dark
We went from listening on the radio to black & white TVs to color technology
Today, driving through the Ft. Pitt tunnels at night into a city of bright lights.
Things come and go and technology changes, but Pittsburgh remains our pride
Written By: The Residents of North Hills Health and Rehab
Date: March 7, 2016

Beaver Valley Nursing and Rehab

Canning Shelves
There weren't so many big malls and traffic, that's true
Albert worked two and a half acres from sun up to sun down
There was lots to do... peas, beans, onions just grew and grew
The photo in black and white detailing how the onions were one pound
We all had lots of people to feed and had enough all winter long
Our canning cellars had many shelves full with sealed mason jars
Looking back at it all now I guess our world has grown too and by far
Yet it's still the same. Eating veggies every day is the best you can do!

The Smell of Hope
The thought of liver and onions in the frying pan with butter, oh...
That delicious smell making me hungry! Is there anything better?!
Better for our families. Better than it was for us than it was before
Mothers and wives handing over packed lunch buckets at the door
Men walking to mills and mines for work and children walking to school
Taylor's Dairy in Beaver County delivered the milk staying nice and cool
When the steel mills shut down, our teachers taught, "What is hope?!"
And hope grew dreams that grew jobs to work! Yeah, this is no joke!!
Written By: The Residents of Beaver Valley Nursing and Rehab
Date: March 10, 2016

Willow Heights

The Poetry of Radio Baseball

Reading the poetry of poets explains how the world does work
Often, we think about these things during the night when we get up
Thoughts for the evening are windows to see outside ourselves
Us kids didn't have television, so radio listening was our big perk
Jazz and poetry: One begets the other, spawning an imagination
Rosey Rowswell and Bob Prince entertaining us calling those games
They were so good at it you felt right at the baseball park that day
Then women weren't as crazy for baseball as the women are today
We listened because men were listening and now it is another way
Maybe how boring high school poetry was compared to modern-day

Love's the Secret Ingredient

When we were 14, we all had skinny legs then, what happened?!
I felt so humiliated when my cousins called me "spindle-shankles"
Others who wore ponytails could find their hair dipped in ink wells
Us women persevered through an awful lot of demanding stances
We had it hard back then and so we rarely ever took any chances...
When the garden would ripen we picked and canned that same day
We had to because we needed food for family from winter until May
Karen remembers her mother even canned deer meat, work always!
My hubby and I worked together to can like we were really starving
And well nowadays, we can just get what we need at the Giant Eagle
But, still today, like then, a good neighbor will bring canned peaches
Home made is quite an undertaking with "love" as a main ingredient!
Written By: The Residents of Willow Heights
Date: March 10, 2016

Senior Center at the Beaver Valley Mall

It's a Big Party Day

From the moment I set eyes on these seniors at the Beaver Valley Mall
I could tell that today with these card, pool and bingo playing folks, we'd
have a ball!
Bob offered me a $5.00 bill for my green hat so he too could start party-
ing right away!
And, some woman came up to me, "Today is St. Patty's Day and I have
on a green
Pittsburgh Penguins practice jersey my son bought at a fundraiser
for me
My last name is Smith and that's what they put on the back and, hey, I'm
number one!"
This place was sure hopping and it wasn't even noon — with some old
"Irish Rose" tune —
Great background music as we were working the room collecting words
for poetry
Now you can't get confused when you hear what this Pinochle Club had
to say today,
"It's a big party day! — Yeah, I'm not even Irish, but, hey, what's there
not to like, right?!
Another woman was telling everyone how her Leprechaun was playing
tricks on her by
leaving her a rabbit made of balloons to wait for wearing on her head,
on Easter Sunday
But she defiantly said, "It's green, so it's okay for me to be wearing here
on St. Patty's
Day!" The consensus at the Beaver Valley Mall was Christmas; may be
the only happier holiday!!
Written By: The Beaver Valley Mall Seniors
Date: March 17, 2016

Willow Lane

Cheese Crackers
Cheese crackers. This poem has backers. And, is shy of hackers.
Like Hunky music?! It's Slovak, Polish, and Hungarian all mixed up!
I wish I could go back in time to see that place I was back in, in 1935.
I was learning how to speak Slovak on Polish Hill above the steel mills.
Today, March 2016, it's the 200th anniversary for the city of Pittsburgh.
They're gonna open a time capsule! Will they find our cheese crackers?!

Time Capsule (for Pittsburgh 200 Years from Now)
Learning is never finished; architecture on the top of the Cathedral of Learning -
University of Pittsburgh's crown jewel with its authentic nationalities classrooms
Symbols of our Pittsburgh, a bottle of Heinz 57 Ketchup and an old rotary phone,
Miniature models of trolley cars and their tracks with a bell that rings, "ding, ding!"
Of course, there has to be a baseball playing card for Pirates' Roberto Clemente...
And a picture of the Incline overlooking the football stadium everyone loves to see
Written By: The Residents of Willow Lane
Date: March 18, 2016

Cumberland Crossing Manor

When It's Turning Spring
We grew up and are all from different neighborhoods of Pittsburgh:
Like Millvale, Squirrel Hill, East Liberty, Oakland, and the North Side,
Plus Blawnox, West View, Spring Hill and Garden too, Etna, Sharpsburg.
Wherever we did reside we could tell it was turning into springtime
by...
Flowers that started growing and the awaited warm breezes that did
arrive.
Spring would soon bloom into summer with a good feeling of being
alive
Even the birds seem to communicate a new thing, "chirp, chirp,"
chirping
It's that joyfulness and magic of a full garden where we all are picnicking
Harvesting fresh fruits and vegetables --- Grapes, radishes and cherries,
Tomatoes, apples, rhubarb all cut-up and some sliced for hot tasty pies!!

Universities and World Series
Spring brings baseball season along with yellow daffodils, red roses,
Purple lilacs and violets and blue iris and those fabulous colors of tulips
Where both Carnegie Mellon University & the University of Pittsburgh
sit
Once there stood the glory of our Pittsburgh Pirates there at Forbes
Field
In 1960, while flowers bloomed brightly, our baseball team delivered a
win -
Universities wowing the world with research while the Pirates close the
deal
The story of leading universities and our Pirates winning the World
Series -
It's prideful history of our city of Pittsburgh - in Oakland - up in the city's
hills

Written By: The Residents of Cumberland Crossing Manor
Date: March 21, 2016

Rochester Manor and Villa

It's No Picnic Out There Anymore
We are familiar with the letters PPG and seeing
a pensioner's picnic for Pittsburgh Plate Glass.
Allegheny Ludlum had a Christmas thing for kids.
In those days they spoke Latin celebrating mass
But they don't speak Latin in mass any more...
I had a brother who worked at that Phoenix Glass.
National Electric had a company picnic for whoever
on this fun day an employee wanted to bring along,
Where we all sat around, danced, ate, and sang songs.
And I worked at Page Steel & Wire Co. / American
Chain & Cable Company. And me, I worked at LTV.
The days of Franklin Avenue being busy all day long
With the town, Aliquippa, once known as Woodlawn -
Devastated by gigantic standing steel mills all gone.
18,000 men and women blocked from entering its doors.
Plus, they don't speak Latin celebrating mass anymore.
Written By: The Residents of Rochester Manor & Villa
Date: March 23, 2016

Independence Court

Special Mother's Love
Appeals to the goodness in all of us
- a mother's love -
She fears she can't even give enough.
Mothers want to see their children succeed.
However, sometimes it's hard to cut the apron strings
- We know it. We see.
Mothers have faith and believe!
The simple fact of fate is the truth in the words,
"This too shall pass." So effective when spoken
From your mother at the right time and the right place.

Lucky To Be Here With You
Boys and men have adoration for their mothers.
And, men have adoration for their lovers.
Seeing is believing...
Girls have adoration for their fathers too.
It's that love - fairy tales that come true.
All I know is I love being here with you!
Written By: The Residents of Independence Court, Monroeville
Date: March 24, 2016

Canterbury Place

Canterbury Tales
I was debating whether or not to attend
-the poetry therapy workshop-
I was afraid maybe I couldn't find a rhyme
And, I was another, an unsure poet friend
-Glad you shared the changes of the time.
We are never too old to learn something...
WE SHOULD HOPE NOT!
The Crawford Grill — on The Hill. ("You know,
everyplace seems on the hill when you're from
flat land Ohio," said one resident participant), a
venue featuring Jazz music that brought change
People came to listen to it from way far away
Artists from Pittsburgh knew what music to play
By an improvisational instinct that bit and stung
Those writers and poets who had silver tongue
Written By: The Residents of Canterbury Place
Date: March 30, 2016

ManorCare

Nothing Better
Making blackberry jelly!
I picked the berries and made the jelly myself.
Yes, I did. I loved it. Nothing better than home-made
blackberry jelly! Well, and then, Grandma always
had some bacon cooking in a pan about every day!
Bacon, every day for breakfast! Sliced tomatoes
And not just for spaghetti — simply placed on a plate
Some of us ate them with bacon, salt, and pepper and
jelly if anyone wants it...Don't forget your hot biscuits!

The Whole Truth
When I was a little kid, Clemente
lived down the street from me.
That made me feel good! Actually,
that made the whole entire city
feel good that we had Clemente!
We love Pittsburgh. We love our Pirates.
And we love #21 Roberto Clemente.
Amen!! He was a good baseball player.
He was a special man. Yes, he was.
His career was short and sweet.
But we still get chills over Clemente!
Written By: The Residents of ManorCare, Shadyside
Date: March 31, 2016

CHAPTER 3

APRIL

Canterbury Place

Bone Soup
Friends and family...
Selective canning...
The knowledge flows like a fountain.
Muslin to wrap hot mason jar.
Seals so hot, muslin to protect hands.
Do you remember the root beer we made?
I'd never change our childhood for today.
I enjoyed our homemade ice-cream!
Butcher's bones we boiled every day.
Games we kids used to play...
Friends & family are our good memories.

New Year's Tradition
My mother and dad made the kraut.
They had it fresh and made it with lots of salt.
Others had sauerkraut and with kielbasa too...
Layering meat with lard kept it all winter long.
Lard by the yard after New Year's Day.
It was a tradition not just for an everyday.
My mother would always say,
"Don't eat chicken on New Year's because
You'll be scratching all year long!"...
Written By: The Residents of Canterbury Place
Date: April 1, 2016

North Hills Health and Rehab

Easter Sunday of Past
Women wore spring hats and white gloves
We shopped to go to mass on Easter Sunday
Patent leather shoes and soft "kid gloves"...
Yellow, white, pink, purple – all pastel dresses
Men wore white shirts, nice suits, and bow-ties
We were celebrating that Jesus had come alive!
Easter lilies and Easter baskets filled with candy
Sitting in pews at church fixing the gloves on hand
We all went to church as a family to stay and pray
After church we loved to feast on special Easter ham

That Far on a Street Car
I know somebody that loved to shop!
While men took streetcars to work, we'd hop on
Trolley cars to go to lunch at Murphy's and shop
J.C. Penney, Horns, Gimbels, Kaufman's, Frank & Cedar
Boggs & Buhl on the North Side and Jenkins Arcade downtown
--Rosenbaum's and Saks Fifth Avenue were around---
They all had "bargain basements" to be found—
A pick-me- up treat was Cherry Coke at Sun Drug Pharmacy
And for a special day we may have had veal at Tambellini's
Written By: The Residents of North Hills Health and Rehab
Date: April 4, 2016

McMurray Hills Nursing and Rehab

That's the Way It Goes
Cheese crackers - a food that matters.
Similarly, like a good pitcher - against good batters.
Grand slam! This could be enough to win the game!!
We sure like our chances with our Pittsburgh Pirates.
We make the other teams' offense and defense splatter.
Winning the World Series gives you Ritz cracker fame;
Every goal that matters - Over the wall =Just the same

We Miss the Duke
"Check on the wagons ---
Get those wagons going!"
He'd say.
His good character
never changed
and always
stayed the same.
He didn't play Moses
but, well, had a smile
like a dozen red roses.
Written By: The Residents of McMurray Hills Nursing and Rehab
Date: April 5, 2016

Marian Manor

Take Me Out to the Old Ball Game
I lived across from Forbes Field, in
a rooming-house in Oakland on the hill.
"My father," said a daughter
"saw Jackie Robinson play there."
When playing the Pirates, his team
didn't have anxiety or fear. They had
the Pittsburgh Pirates number man!
But don't count out
our beloved Bucco's!!
As our city's baseball legacy goes,
The Pirates have given us plenty of cheer;
"Peanuts, popcorn, Cracker Jacks!!"
All year, we would be waiting to hear
the attendants yell out those words.
While Clemente's big play made many at
a summer's ball game jump and spill their beer
Written By: The Residents of Marian Manor
Date: April 6, 2016

Cranberry Place

We Grew the Lord's Bounty

We would grow corn, peas,
tomatoes and green beans
Spinach, onions, carrots,
rhubarb, apples and peaches
--- Peaches on trees
And grapes on vines
To make grape jelly and wine!
Those fruit trees,
So good for making hot pies!
All those home-made things,
Were done with love we realize

Ball Game

At Forbes Field, men wore sporty caps, top hats, suits with ties
Women had their hair fixed, wore dresses and pearls with such style
This was everyday life in Pittsburgh like that Life Magazine cover photo
In the bleachers drinking Coca-Cola in glass bottles, eating Cracker
Jacks,
Hot dogs with relish, chili, onions, Heinz 57, and all the cotton candy
colored
Pink and blue! What a glorious view indeed with the setting sun at our
backs
Written By: The Residents of Cranberry Place
Date: April 8, 2016

West Hills Health and Rehab

We Still Hate Bad Winter Months
Salt.
Lots of salt to melt
the ice and snow.
It was tough in
Pittsburgh winter months
when the cold wind would blow.
We still
had to walk in all winter weather to our schools;
I like to sleigh ride with you
But sometimes even that
was just too cold to do too ---
Good grief!
We almost
killed ourselves
on those sleds! So hard to guide,
sliding down a hill going here and there
And you just never knew ---
might end up in the creek soaking wet
Lucky not to be frozen blue!!
Written By: The Residents of West Hills Health and Rehab
Date: April 9, 2016

The Pines

I Sing Coal Miner's Daughter
"I lived it every day, "she said. "Every day"...
Yeah, my family used to pickle green beans in summer
She continues, "We had to grow because we couldn't pay
Spring, summer, and fall, we did it all to eat through the winter
We had to fence in the cattle — that fence gave me a mean splinter
I was a coal miner's daughter and, I still do, love to sing that song."

That's the Way It Is
We had rhubarb pie that sure was oh-so delicious
Every year, that rhubarb plant came up and we picked it
We would can it and all year have us fresh rhubarb pie
Funny thing, that plant would give without us doing anything
Even funnier, we kept all those "canned goods" in mason jars
And, even funnier, we stored them all in what we would call
The fruit cellar, canning cellar, cold cellar, and the coal cellar
Written By: The Residents of The Pines, Mt. Lebanon
Date: April 12, 2016

Willow Heights

Good and Strong People

The Singer Ice Company put a skating rink off Chartiers Avenue
It was a real innovation at the time, as there weren't many around
These river towns of South Western, PA, were so busy and bustling
That's the way it was in town before they tore the steel mills down
Despite, we thank God every day that we place our two feet on the floor
We all sure take a lot for granted, so try and be thankful at the door

Swings and Things

My father and uncle sat on the porch and listened to the ballgame
On the radio — on the front porch of our home in McKeesport —
So, whatever happened to sitting outside on the front porch swings?!
I found an old book on Rosey Rowswell, announcer of baseball kings!
About 10 years ago now, I found that book.
I'm originally from Swissvale
The guys would go together to Pirate games when not in the steel mills
Pitchers on our porch of ice tea and lemonade watching those passers-by
One guy used to walk past our front porches and smell what's cooking!...
It was nice back then before backyard patios when we walked sidewalks
Hearing similar families gathered on porches listening to the Pirate games
Jumping rope as kids — front porch was the hub — always keeping entertained
Written By: The Residents of Willow Heights
Date: April 14, 2016

Willow Lane

Our Neighborhood

Pittsburgh's pierogies eating population...
Ethnic foods of our city sparks conversations
In fact, each catholic nationality had its own church for worship
And inside the basement for the community center, Heinz 57 ketchup
No matter what nationality we had festivals for all to participate
With parishioners, family, and friends we gathered and, boy, we ate

DanceLand USA

He sits around and talks about it all day
She pinned a rose upon him at DanceLand USA
They danced the two-step-Polka by the merry-go-round
Now they say they were fortunate it never rained on their parade
A lot of Pittsburgh girls met their husbands there looking around
She saw him, pinned him to show she liked him and kissed his lips
All we did at West View Park was dance, dance, dance from our hips
Written By: The Residents of Willow Lane
Date: April 15, 2016

Cumberland Crossing

Glorious Spring
It is a lovely spring day
Looking forward to summer
The geese have returned
We know next comes May
Yellow daffodils are abound
Along with tulips all around
Birds flying and beautifully singing
Baby birdies way up in their nests
Waiting on their mothers for food
Spring Sunday church bells ringing
After mass, we eat and we do rest
Springtime sure elevates our mood
Written By: The Residents of Cumberland Crossing
Date: April 18, 2016

Beaver Eldercare

Love

There are different kinds of love...
A love for a mother, sibling, pet or dove...
The love for church and patron saints
Love that comes before it's too late.
Your love for your spouse until the end
Even if he's a louse! We realize and allow mistakes.
Maybe it's okay for a father to prevent a second date.

Life in the 40's in Beaver County

In Beaver County it has been tradition to care for a garden
Gardening as a community as we have now in Beaver Falls
West Aliquippa had a fertile little island off the Ohio River banks
Was a wooden bridge to walk on to get to the community garden
Muslin covered plants in early chilly spring until the earth thawed
When not working in the mill we gardened and canned together...
And the "milk-man" delivery was essential in bad winter weather
Well, and then, our stories go back to when it was a nickel for gas
Written By: The Residents of Beaver ElderCare
Date: April 22, 2016

Forbes Center for Rehabilitation and Healthcare

A Pinch of This and a Dash of That
Peeling bushels of peaches for canning
In mason jars stored in cupboards on shelves
Mother canned everything and put wax on top of the jelly
If you came to our house, you got a jar of peach preserve
Potatoes and homemade rolls. Oh, how I miss those days
I loved it. Yep, every kind of fruit and every kind of vegetable
Whoa, how those rolls and the bread just melted in your mouth
A pinch of this and a dash of that -- we never really measured!
Gosh, I miss biscuits made by Grandma with chicken and greens

Old Pittsburgh Travels
Once your family and your vehicle would fit on the Incline
Up on Mt. Washington in Allentown down to the South Side
Then I prayed that "75" street car wouldn't be late to catch
Cause I didn't want to be late for work on Montefiore's watch
Written By: The Residents of Forbes Center for Rehabilitation and
Healthcare
Date: April 25, 2016

Forbes Center for Rehabilitation and Healthcare

Pittsburgh Spirit

No matter what city you may find yourself in...

Whether it's the Pittsburgh Pirates, Steelers or Penguins

And, let's not forget our Pittsburgh River Hounds, we like wins!

Big wins like Stanley Cups, Lombardi Trophies, and World Series rings

When Pittsburgh wins, it's like Woodstock has come all over the town

"The Bus" Jerome Bettis, Franco's Immaculate Reception, and then

Mario Lemieux "The Elvis of Hockey" and Pirate Roberto Clemente

And the Pirate Parrot, the Penguins' Iceburg and Steeley McBeam

And those Pittsburgh Pirate game Pierogi races are surely fan faves

Written By: The Residents of Forbes Center for Rehabilitation and Healthcare

Date: April 25, 2016

ManorCare

Chicken Soup for the Mind
We write
poetry that's chicken soup for the mind
We find out
our memories currently help us find
the diamond series of our years —
going back in time to our days here
Chicken soup for the mind —
going back in time
You can have chicken soup at midnight
but don't let your mind too far out of sight
Don't let your noodle become a Google
(use your head instead)

Cookie Lady
Cookie Lady entertains us all day long
Recites poetry and on an organ sings us songs
Sing us that song on how to get on along
Cookie Lady, sung us that song all day long
What a way Cookie Lady got to be on KDKA
That's Pittsburgh Today Live---
Come on, Cookie Lady sing how we come alive
Giving us her fury bingo winnings and her time
Written By: The Residents of ManorCare, GreenTree
Date: April 26, 2016

Independence Court

Making History
Mustard plaster— a home-made
recipe for sickness of the chest
Made with mustard & muslin to aid
So us sick kids could get some rest
Tomato juice — something else fresh
To the mustard and pickles we ate...
Jellies made with strawberries, grapes, and peaches
Preserves made with blueberries
And we also made and ate many fruit pies
The days we toiled under those blue skies

Sundaes on Stools
A pharmacy by my home
They served
Cherry Coke
We never felt too alone
Friends, family, and kinfolk
Coca-Cola was the real deal
It was a cure-all syrup...
Sitting on stools like wheels
Written By: The Residents of Independence Court, Monroeville
Date: April 27, 2016

Elmcroft

Tomatoes and Peppers
Tomatoes and peppers
...Jams and Jellies...
Sauerkraut, wedding soup
String beans....
Elderberry, we recall
We canned all kinds of stuff
We made homemade sausage
"Waste not want not," we'd say.
The best jelly ever ---
Better than the stores
A lot of work but
We would do it again now
And do it even more ---
Written By: The Residents of Elmcroft, Allison Park
Date: April 28, 2016

Elmcroft

Spring Has Sprung
Lettuce was the first to arrive
Stuck indoors all winter long
Like the first spring buds, we're alive
Building nests, laying eggs, singing songs
Birds and bees and squirrels, rabbits and peas
All these things tell us it is spring indeed
March brings green colors and soon to be
Caterpillars making time as butterflies
Hummingbirds come into view and fluttering
Gone as fast as these lovely spring days

Little White Socks
The little white socks and shoes
Shopped for Eater Sunday mass
We went from black patent leather
To the shiny bright white for church
Bonnets and ribbons and brimmed hats
All those petticoats starched...
Made for itchy but full dresses
Those days big stores had lunch counters
All for Easter Sunday shopping in March
Written By: The Residents of Elmcroft, Chippewa
Date: April 29, 2016

CHAPTER 4

MAY

Wexford House

Transfixed by the Radio
Our poems
They come assembled together
Like the old books read and bound in leather
In the den with a fire transfixed by the radio
Eating popcorn listening to the Lone Ranger
With eyes aglow

Cold Pack Our Fruits
Beets and carrots we grew and peaches
Practically name anything and we grew it
Peppers and tomatoes, blackberries, corn
Cabbage, lettuce, squash, elderberries --
Huckleberries - a word Mark Twain used -is
another name for wild blueberries grown
Peppers, onions, and sausage in a frying pan
Now listen to this, what we do miss is that
Home-made food we adore and want more
Hanging meats downstairs to age and cure
We tighten mason jar lids with rubber bands
Food doesn't spoil when it's cold pack, man!!
Written By: The Residents of Wexford House
Date: May 2, 2016

West Hills Health and Rehab

How You Feelin'?
In Coraopolis "the gossiping paper" was called The Record
A big paper was The Press and now we have the USA Today...
Locally, The Pittsburgh Tribune Review and Pittsburgh Post-Gazette
Our Channel 4 WTAE, Channel 11 WPX1, and Channel 2 KDKA
Either way, we check the weather, obituaries, and sports everyday

Americana
In those Sears catalogs - Ads in the newspapers -
Billboards and advertisements on sides of barns
If you went along and passed Mr. Smith's big old farm
You saw painted Coca-Cola and Mail Pouch Ads
Riding in a car on a hot summer's day listening on
The radio the advertisement for Five Bros Tobacco
For the first time, I realized what a friend was saying..
The summer sky was the color of blueberries in pie
Written By: The Residents of West Hills Health and Rehab
Date: May 3, 2016

Paramount Senior Living

The Yummy Tomato

As fresh tomatoes grew, we
Awaited what we knew was true
True indeed. We'd "can" these and
Soon be making stews and sauces
Pizza and, well, just by themselves.
Now, my granddaughter eats tomatoes,
She eats them with mozzarella cheese.
We, maybe sometimes, ate them plain.
Using only some sea salt and fresh rain.
As rain would fall, we used to see all the
Wonderful plants and vines growing green.
One thing our parents weren't so lenient on
Was being called late at the family dinner table
- "A family that eats together stays together" -
And so we like eating together every single day
The yummy tomato placed by basil both labeled

Pill Box Hat

Even at a Pirates game, women
Wore those kinda "Jackie 0." hats.
But one thing is certainly for sure...
Before you would walk out that door
For Sunday services and mass --
Better have on a nice Sunday hat!!
Written By: The Residents of Paramount Senior Living, Peters Township
Date: May 4, 2016

Marian Manor

I Got Chills
I was there in a private box
It was the year 1960 in Pittsburgh
It had been 35 years since the last
A World Series Win was well in the past
Working for the steel fabrication company
I was there when Bill Mazeroski scored
Number 9 "Maz" at bat and he won us the game
The Pittsburgh Pirates beat New York
The N.Y. Yankees lost that day 3 to 4!!
Still beating us in total hits and runs
Our Bucco's overcame the odds
October in 1960 and in Pittsburgh
We were the underdogs who won

Spring Song
Bristling bushy brush
Listen to birds sing
It's spring
What a time to be alive
When rose blooms arrive
Memorial Day Parades
The neighborhood kids
Gathered with their dimes
At the lemonade stands
Written By: The Residents of Marian Manor
Date: May 5, 2016

Grace Manor at North Park

Preserving the Ping

When canning, if you didn't hear a ping
You had to do it over until it was done right
Until it did seal. That was, of course, the deal
And If it wasn't kosher, well, it didn't go either
The strawberries were the center of attention
Jam so good it could be sauce on ice cream
Now that is sure some real, real good eating
Make sure we label our pies when at a dinner
That way we'll know how to identify the winner

Save It

Don't throw your Sears catalogs away!
Well, back in the day!! Sure, and now, I say...
We lived on a farm in Armstrong County.
We had no electricity - lights from kerosene
At age 8 or 9, I walked about 5 miles to school
Zero running water. A pump-house and coal stove
And, we saved every Sears catalog. Know what
I mean... Never throw that way! You save it!!!
In Lawrenceville, our luxury was only reading it.
Written By: The Residents of Grace Manor at North Park
Date: May 5, 2016

North Hills Health and Rehab

Mill Hunky

Buying everybody at the bar a drink!
My mill-hunky husband who do you think?!
If I don't catch him, he'll spend the whole paycheck
Wondering why he gets the broom?! What the heck!

Instead of in Rumble Seats

While some were out at the clubs or bars
With records playing on the record player
If nothing else to do or we were too young
We used to have fun dancing in the kitchen
The polka, two-step, waltz and in the rumble seats
"You ain't going nowhere dressed like that!"...
Mom and dad set the dress-code and the curfew
And liked it best when we dressed for ice skating
Written By: The Residents of North Hills and Rehab
Date: May 9, 2016

The Pines

Jam & Jelly
Wax on top of homemade jelly
That sealed its container shut
Jelly doesn't have the fruit in it
It is just the juice
Jam has the fruit
It's all mashed-up
"It must be jelly 'cause jam,
don't shake like that!!"...
But it still got the wax

Family Tradition
Horseradish freshly grated made our eyes cry
Though well worth it spread on sliced beef
And horseradish turned red from juice of beets
Baked special at Easter time
Paska bread we'd make
Inside its hollow space we
Placed many colored eggs
This was tradition and was and
still is our family ways
Written By: The Residents of The Pines, Mt. Lebanon
Date: May 10, 2016

Baldwin Health Center

Her Words
"My husband had a yellow convertible.
I wanted to shoot him every day...
The girls tried jumping in — in a big way!!
Give your ear to God and the rest is mine!"

The Root Cellar
You gotta keep it cool
Like the root cellar do
Like the basement and
Fruit, coal and cold cellars do
Pickled beets, apples and corn
All the things we used to store
Fresh blackberries we'd eat for days
Passing time fishing with earth worms
Canning and fishing and keeping it cool
In summertime, that's how we used to do
Written By: The Residents of Baldwin Health Center
Date: May 11, 2016

ManorCare

Steel Mills
From Frazier Street
I could see
All of the men
on Second Street
going to work
My father was a coal miner
God bless him
Men entering and exiting
the big mills with home-made
sandwiches and coffee in lunch pails
Memories unwind like concrete in sets
of steps down the hill to work in the mill
Going home was a big deal with all those
steps to climb. And all after a hard day's
work inside rusted confines with red hot fires

Grandma's Hands
Grandma did the gardening
And was matriarch in our family
We learned a way of life and how to be
Coconut, pumpkin, pecan, sweet potato
Oh, be mine, pineapple-upside-down cake
The strudel she baked was the best made
Well, sweets and all foods she made great
Written By: The Residents of Manor Care, Pittsburgh
Date: May 11, 2016

Ross Hill Retirement

Victory Gardens
Neighbors were sure not aloof like they can be today
Everybody watched a kid when they were out to play
During the War, we all visited and worked in the soil
"Victory Garden"- to grow and preserve garden produce
It was a way for us families and troops to be able to eat all year
We didn't have $400.00 sneakers — lucky to have one pair
And we were happy with mother's flower-sack-slips to wear

Frank and Cedar
On the first floor of Frank & Cedar in downtown Pittsburgh
For those who could afford not to bargain on the basement floor
Sales ladies would put their hands in stockings showing a seam
We may have those on at one of the dances at Kennywood
While grandmothers sat at the picnic tables with packed baskets
Was back in time when public schools required girls wear dresses
Written By: The Residents of Ross Hill Retirement
Date: May 12, 2016

Cranberry Place

The Growl of Rin-Tin-Tin

Movies, TV, radio, and comic books
Hollywood sure could set those hooks
Horror movies like Nightmare on Elm Street
We wish the Hulk would appear and be green
And defeat the villain who hooks us with fear
All of us dream of having our own Rin-Tin-Tin
Tinsel Town makes us big stars who could win
Most of the time from the start won our hearts

King and Queen of the Jungle

Did Tarzan have Cheetah
before there was a Jane
Cheetah, Tarzan's best friend,
He was a chimpanzee
They swung from vines limb to
limb and tree to tree
They built a house for a home
when Jane made three
Bamboo and vines they
combined for a neat tree house
And the interior decorating was
indeed done by Jane
Of course, Queen of the Jungle,
Tarzan and Cheetah
King of the Wild with a distinct
yodel as his manly call
Written By: The Residents of Cranberry Place
Date: May 13, 2016

HealthSouth

My Mother in Spring-time
A chapel veil gracing her pretty hair
At mass or service, this is what we'd wear
This was the alternative in place of a hat
Easter bonnets with bows and flowers upon it
We all were proud ladies in the Easter Parade
Men were proud of their ladies too on Easter-Day
And, hey, men cleaned up fine too, count on it

Before There Were Freezers
Boil the mason jar
It can't have bacteria in it
If you plan on waxing it rather—
Than using a rubber band lid
The paraffin will also provide a seal
50 pounds of plums in mason jars filled
Our mothers canned fruits like peaches
And canned tomatoes and other veggies
Written By: The Residents of HealthSouth, Sewickley
Date: May 16, 2016

ManorCare

Whipple Wine
Up on Polish Hill?!...
I know Polish Hill N'at!
Go across the bridge
And there's what you call it
N'at - There's a brewery and
Restaurants N'at and they
Make pierogies and other home-
made stuff N'at O.K. home-
made wine - Whipple Wine,
Made from dandelions and
You can drink a few glasses
But you're on the couch cushions
For the rest of the night - Up on
Polish Hill N'at ain't coming down

Pickles, Jellies, and Hungry Bellies
There are lots of things to can and pickle
Like cucumbers mother made when I was little
The key is to try the canned goods and not be fickle
Hot peppers hung dried for months can make you cry
Quince jelly made from quince bushes growing to the sky
We don't see much quince now but it tastes similar to a pear
Nowadays, Mike's Packing House, Washington, Pa., Lincoln Hill
Has hot and sweet pepper jelly and, like mom, home-made everything
Corn-Cobb jelly, red or green gooseberry jellies make us sing..
"We love home-made jellies - love those jellies in our hungry bellies"
Written By: The Residents of ManorCare, Peters Twp.
Date: May 17, 2016

Independence Court

Manners Please
Sit up straight
Manners at the table
All kids should be able
To help with the dishes
Or maybe their wishes
Aren't so easily granted
Manners are good
Character and manners
Both really do matter
Not where you were born

Elbow Grease
Before there
were dishwashers
There was "Mom"...
Soapy water and Brillo pads.
Some of us don't have one yet
We still rely on our elbow grease.
Go on, let us say our peace...
A piece of mind we find like
Corsages every year at Easter
Written By: The Residents of Independence Court, Monroeville
Date: May 18, 2016

Independence Court

Reminiscing

Amos and Andy, The Lone Ranger,
Fibber McGee and Molly, The Shadow
... "The Shadow Knows"...
When to listen to the radio
Actual shows read over the radio
Broadcasted over the air-waves
Before there was black and white TV
And, the Honeymooners, Jackie Gleason
... "To the moon, Alice"...
I Love Lucy, Dick Van Dyke,
Twilight Zone, The Lone Ranger, when yes
We finally got to see Tonto and Silver on TV

Emily Says

If you didn't go to church,
You weren't going anywhere.
If the phone rang during dinner,
Whoever answered it wasn't a winner.
Forks on the dinner plate's left side
with the bread plate. And on the right
side the water and wine glasses and
Spoons and knives... Of course, if
At a party, it was a must we would wait
For the good hostess first before we ate.
According to Emily Post and her book
"The Complete Guide to Modern Manners"
Written By: The Residents of Independence Court, Monroeville
Date: May 18, 2016

ManorCare

Foggy Morning Sunny Day

Good morning! Sun is shining today
It's so nice to see blue skies in May
Mornings like this remind us of vacation
Foggy at first but once the fog burns away
A beautiful start to an easy vacation day
If we see a foggy mountain we can count on
A good chance it's a cool dry sunny sky day

Thirsty Then and Now

It was a nickel or a dime for a glass of lemonade
Through time, man, inflation, is rough in 2016 today
The kids on the corner with their lemonade stands
It's 50 cents per one glass that the kids now demand
And for charity, it could be up to a whole one dollar bill
However, this is for a good cause for those who are ill
Written By: The Residents of ManorCare, GreenTree
Date: May 19, 2016

ManorCare

Fifth Avenue Shadyside
Looking in a mirror doesn't necessarily mean
That the mirror is telling your life's story...
I knew nothing of her five children and husband
And the pies she baked and the dinners made
The broken legs, tears, and smiles of a family
As I am passing by in a truck looking at luck
And the lines of her face and on Fifth Avenue
With the old mansions with six window views
I wonder if she knows who she really is inside
And in this poem I have her down as of age 62

Nothing but Love
If you have a child...
And you make food for that child
Two times a day for 18 years =
That turns out to be 13,140 meals
Meals that you prepared for them
Now those numbers are really wild
Nothing but love — love for the child
Written By: The Residents of ManorCare, Shadyside
Date May 19, 2016

Forbes Center for Rehabilitation and Health

Railways Restaurant
In the back of Murphy's Five & Dime...
The smell of hamburgers got me every time with
Some fresh-cut potato chips and nuts and an open door
Letting in blowing freezing cold wind and "to go" or "dine in"
You'll be back again and again for the best around in town
Filled up with Pepsi and Coke at home, we joined the "party line"

The Old Juke Box
Smokey Joe's Cafe - so smoky back in the day
There were juke boxes on top of every table - The way
It happened was you dropped a dime for a song that rhymed
To sing with your boy and girl friends - Oh, yeah, what a time
... "I found my thrills - on Blueberry Hill" - Fats Domino...
Syrupy blueberry pancakes, home fries, hot coffee or cocoa
Aretha Franklin, and that Johnny Cash and a cold six pack to go
Written By: The Residents of Forbes Center for Rehabilitation and Health
Date: May 20, 2016

Forbes Center for Rehabilitation and Health

The Sunshine

The sun shines on so brightly...
It lets me know Christ is in my heart.
I love the sun. It reminds me there's a creator.
And I hope the sun shines when we go to Wal-Mart.
The sun inspires me and I desperately need slippers.
The good times like a 1st place hat make me smile.
Game day with pizza and dancing on top of sun shine

Biscuits and Grits

Morning sun cracks the night's dark pan
Big starry skies - round as the eggs frying
We put butter, salt, and pepper on top of grits
Oatmeal's different, so no sugar, like on top of it
Grits and sardines like down in Alabama, wham!
How's that?! Good old home cooking with white,
yellow, red, purple, Spanish and sweet onions, hey,
Every morning we got dark roast coffee to percolate
Biscuits and grits, a dish with lots of butter on top of it
Written By: The Residents of Forbes Center for Rehabilitation and Health
Date: May 20, 2016

Vincentian De Marillac

Mom's Pickle Lilly
Green tomatoes and onions
Little pieces of sweet peppers
Pickling spice and minced garlic
Basil and some white vinegar
This group is known for Pickle Lilly
Ah, what a sweet, sweet dish...
It reminds us of mother's wish
We'd make sure to pass it along
Honor as a recipe we remember
Or even shared in a poem song

Kleenex and Bobby Pins
When we were downtown
We had gloves, hats, and dresses
Stockings with seams and nice shoes
Didn't leave the house playing around
And when in God's house no messes
In the pews, we dressed with respect
Today, anything seems to go anywhere
We remember days of our confessions
Never wore shorts to mass nor did dare
Written By: The Residents of Vincentian De Marillac
Date: May 23, 2016

New Hope

We Want One This Year
With five World Series wins and rings
The Pirates winning one this year we'd sing
Oh how sweet this blessed sixth victory is
Our song so right for that "pop" show-biz
Dismantled Mickie Mantle's career with 1960 win
Let's Go Bucco's 2016 is the time to win a series again

West View Park
Sights and sounds of West View Park
Bedazzling our eyes and ears after dark
Dancing hearing Tommy Dorsey's clarinet and bands
Piano, saxophone, trombone — drummer, Jean Krupa, and
Another player, Guy Lombardo, played every New Year's Eve
Ringing in we all chimed in to help him sing "Auld Lang Syne"
Screams from the Ferris-Wheel and roller coasters; what a time
Written By: The Residents of New Hope Personal Care Home
Date: May 24, 2016

Eldercrest Nursing Center

Going to Kennywood Again
West View and White Swann
These parks are all gone now
Idlewild Park still in Ligonier but how
Really none are as good as Kennywood
We're going again to Kennywood in June
And, let me tell you, it's none too soon...
Round and round the merry-go-round goes
First kisses we'd steal at "The Old Mill"
Not just on Fats Domino's "Blueberry Hill"
Hungry for some fries; try the Potato Patch
Fried to perfection with toppings unmatched

Tenner Shoes
Pittsburghese doesn't say sneakers
We call them tenner shoes and ours
Back in the day were Converse All-Stars
Black or white canvas Chuck Taylors...
Might've cost us $16 and God forbid they got lost
Well, nowadays you may pay $400 for high-tops
Who the heck and why pay that high of a cost
Written By: The Residents of Eldercrest Nursing Center
Date: May 24, 2016

Beaver Eldercare

Dandelion Wine
Dandelions for miles covering green grass
So many bright yellow dots on our green lawn
Beaming golden sunshine in pink and purple dawn
Early in the morning when they are fresh at last
To make dandelion wine you pick green, not the flower
And if you drink five glasses, you'll be drunk in 5 hours

Summertime Picnic
We did oh so well together packing our picnic baskets
We even brought cards, horseshoes, and badminton rackets
Playing baseball was swell for us boys and us girls remember
The echoing green grass and leaves and little ones twirling...
Watermelon, honeydew, cantaloupe, pears, peaches and shiny
apples — home-made baked cookies, sandwiches, and candy swirls
Sounds of our conversations and laughter canvassing the big park
Written By: The Residents of Beaver Eldercare
Date: May 25, 2016

Willow Heights

Memorial Day
We salute the Stars and Stripes
We sing the Star-Spangled Banner
Some of us in uniform playing bag pipes
Yearly, we do this together in-memoriam
One week sitting in high school at 12 Noon
Next the Battle of Normandy 6th of June

Memorial Day Parade
It does make us all so proud
Rifles exploding, sounding out loud
Reactions to our Memorial parades
Throwing candy and confetti in the street
The man in uniform marching to the beat
Of Yankee Doodle Dandy in the May heat
Written By: The Residents of Willow Heights
Date: May 26, 2016

Beaver Valley Nursing and Rehab

War Everyday

Why do we like Memorial Day?... The
holiday parade and, well, we like eating
hot dogs and riding in Chevrolet's
Done-up decorated with red, white, and blue
For our country's men and women who far away
Fight the battles of being at war every single day

Salute

This Monday is Memorial Day
And for us what an enjoyable way
To honor the soldiers and sailors of war
Airmen and marines overseas on foreign shores
For you, we wave that flag mighty high and wide
It sure is fun celebrating in the U.S.A. with style
Lest we shall forget — which we shall never forget
Written By: The Beaver Valley Nursing and Rehab
Date: May 26, 2016

Rochester Manor & Villa

No Comparison

There's no comparison for kindness
Penny Pots to start plants from seeds
And there's no substitute for pure modesty
Simple keys of life to help one succeed
We shall all grow like our seedling plants
Reaching up towards the sky blue skies
Yet however, even respectful of little ants
No comparison to the perfect summer day
God does give us to guide our humble way

We are the Great City of Pittsburgh

To be a Pittsburgher is so good
We are a true city and our past
does include "mill hunkies", dirt and ash
Smoke and fire; steel city; smoky city
But hard workers that will indeed fill
orders to build the Empire State Bldg.
And win World Wars as we work together
As a melting pot and example to the nation
From our Three Rivers to Point State Park
A gritty pretty city from light until after dark
Written By: The Residents of Rochester Manor & Villa
Date: May 31, 2016

CHAPTER 5

JUNE

Grace Manor at North Park

Car 95
95 Sharpsburg was once a known trolley car
We'd take it from Lawrenceville to West View Park
Our full packed basket for picnicking and that track
Along for the city of Pittsburgh to West View Park
What a delightfully lovely picturesque but bumpy ride
Our escaped grapes in the aisle would roll side to side
Between the grooves of the trolley car's floor, they'd roll
As we got older instead of the grapes dancing in aisles
We would be doing our own dancing at DanceLand USA
We dance side to side the Polkas, moving our eyes

Mimosas on the Blanket
A special wedding gift given for a special day
A sturdy yet charming picnic basket to use to start
Traditions of a new couple and their family's own ways
Molly served mimosas with a big bottle of champagne
Plates supplied inside the basket served Quiche Lorraine
Sitting on a floral blanket at Hartford Acres and listening
To the unique guitar playing and singing of one Mr. B.B. King.
I recollect the couple next to us that night became engaged
He proposed on one knee under the stars with a diamond ring
Written By: The Residents of Grace Manor at North Park
Date: June 2, 2016

Forbes Center for Rehabilitation and Healthcare

Sunday Morning Hymns

When the Saints come marching in
I'll be there for that number and bass run
Everyone around sings on "Amazing Grace"
Either a tear in your eye or smile on your face
Hearing church songs that got it going on...
Inspires that highest and best in all of us...
I can't wait to hear our deacon sing old meter
Hymns like, "Father, I Stretch My Hands to Thee"
Plus this, "I will Trust the Lord" and, yes, in glory

What We Ate at Kennywood

Potato salad, coleslaw, fried chicken, and BBQ
"When is this gonna happen? Because, I'll go!"
For we all used to pack us a picnic basket with
Deviled eggs, pop, pound cakes, pies, and cookies
We would sit on the green lawn and cheer on
Those who had been doing all that good cookin'
Iced teas and lemonade we would be sippin' on
Baked beans, hamburgers, and hot dogs with onion
Then our parents would make us wait half an hour
Sure, a long wait when you don't have say-so power
When all you want to do is be in the seat beside her
Written By: The Residents of Forbes Center for Rehabilitation and Healthcare
Date: June 3, 2016

McMurray Hills Nursing and Rehabilitation

Don't Get Lost In Pittsburgh
Avoid all the Parkways at any cost
Pittsburgh traffic can cause a half day lost
We know back roads in North and South Hills
Crafton's Backbone Road - vehicle's rotating wheels -
Nothing worse than in the heat idling at a standstill
Knowing your way around Pittsburgh is a good deal

He Was Saved
My brother, who's her husband, born on a 3rd floor
Downtown in a building sheltering folks from the storm
March 16th, 1936, the year of the big St. Patty's Day Flood
For his lucky introduction entering Pittsburgh he was adored
He was adored even more as a kid and now still is as her husband
Written By: The Residents of McMurray Hills Nursing and Rehabilitation
Date: June 6, 2016

The Pines

Lightening Bugs
Fireworks big and bright and loud in the sky 4th of July
However, for some, the huge booms brings fright wide-eyed
And instead of fireworks, there are some who have fun on the run
Barefooted little Entomologists fast as lightening catching fireflies

It Was an Interesting Time
My father and relatives, men of age
They shared courage and were brave
After the great flood of 1936 in March
Men cleaned up the ravaged city with heart
The water that peaked at 46 feet devastating
But we rebuilt with innovation and invention
Pittsburgh now receives World Class Ratings
Working at Duquesne Light makes for a fine living
Written By: The Residents of The Pines, Mt. Lebanon
Date: June 6, 2016

Wexford House

The Pennsylvania Polka
Hunky music is music for dancing
Look, her shoulders are moving side to side
Just thinking of that accordion player playing
Babushkas and bright- colored dresses ruffling
Twirling women pounding feet and hands clapping
Out Pennsylvania Polka beats with perfect timing

Radio History
Smelling the popcorn and wood
Hearing the crackling of the fire
It's as if we think we could really
Be back in time of our radio history
Shows with Stella Dallas, Amos and Andy
And listening to The Shadow so intently
Written By: The Residents of Wexford House
Date: June 6, 2016

West Hills Health & Rehab

One Room Schoolhouse
In Oak Forest, there was a schoolhouse
It was one room. Educated a lot of people
We cleaned erasers and we made good friends
Eight grades in a one-room country schoolhouse
From 9 a.m. until the afternoon, five days a week
Every fall, winter, and spring we became like family
Flags, maps, an organ, pictures, and lots of books
Everything in the one room and yes that's all it took

Good Clean Fun
Pennsylvania is a great state for a picnic
Picking blueberries, taking a break from winter work
Swinging on big ropes with seats watching a wild one
Getting loose from volleyball or baseball games to break
My little cousin's glasses that fell into their macaroni salad
We laughed around the campfire; not one at all to be mad at
Written By: The Residents of West Hills Health & Rehab
Date: June 7, 2016

Beaver Eldercare

Proud People of Pittsburgh
You were proud of what you had
We didn't want to be in the cold and mad
We didn't have much, but we had jobs
The budget wasn't a choice but the rule
If you wasted opportunity, you were a fool

Having a Good Time Dancing
Polka hats and blouses with long sleeves
Long skirts that fluttered around like a breeze
Blowing and twirling and dancing around and around
In those days we left our doors unlocked in town
Every Sunday traditional meals cooked all day long
Afterward, we danced to the Pennsylvania Polka song

Picnic Time
Pittsburgh's sunny dry cool summer days
Are certainly far and few between here
Some people in the hollow might well say
From the bottom of the cooler get a beer
Heavy picnic baskets filled with sandwiches
The kids wading in the creek with little fish
Under a canopy of green leaves we shade
Written By: The Residents of Beaver Eldercare
Date: June 8, 2016

ManorCare

Potato Salad, Coleslaw, and Corned Beef
On our picnic table sat...
Bottles of Heinz 57 ketchup, mustard
Hard boiled eggs, a transistor radio or a

Boom-box, bologna sandwiches on our laps
With dill pickles sliced and whole and chips
Wise's barbecue and Herr's plain with dips
Heluva Good! French onion dip plus chipped
Ham from Islay's chipped-chopped-ham
Corn on the cobb with butter and baked beans
Potato salad, coleslaw, and corned beef...
This picnic always hits home like a grand —slam!
Written by: The Residents of ManorCare, Pittsburgh
Date: June 8, 2016

Beatty Pointe Village

When the Garden Is Ripe
Absorbing the perspiration... the muslin fabric...
Gardening is inspiration and for canning, we apply tricks
Peppers, onion, tomatoes, beets, beans, and horseradish
Our fresh garden items grown that make for a yummy dish
Mason jar lids sealed with heat, preserving the peppers' kick
Listening for that ping so we know it's good for cellar storing
Written By: The Residents of Beatty Pointe Village
Date: June 10, 2016

Paramount Senior Living

Remembering Aromas
We remember...We do...That's it
We can see and smell our own ethnic
Foods we consumed and still talk about it
That Paska bread, red cabbage, and beets
Our home-made gnocchi in tomato sauce
Pierogi home-made with potato and cheese
Sautéed onion, butter, salt, and pepper on top
These family memories are never at a loss

The Picnic Basket
In our picnic baskets...
Were flowers that made bouquets
Bright like those in windowsill boxes
Our beer bottles dull brown not green
Father was to be quite clear about this
As direct orders of our home's queen
Written By: The Residents of Paramount Senior Living
Date: June 10, 2016

ManorCare

June Love Bug
June leaves us all too soon
Waking up in a hotel room
After you played the groom
Now beside you is your bride
She becomes your daily pride
And your happy smile is wide
With picnic ants always at your side
And from the hot sun we try to hide
June on our honeymoon carriage ride

Clean Clothes and Green Grass
Nowadays you can hang your sheets outside to dry
But back when we used ice boxes instead of freezers
The Smoky City was too dirty with soot to hang a line
For clothes and linens by Gus and YaYa's in the North Side
Before there was nothing but industrial sites at The Point
And now its space has a fountain and grass never greener
Around Point State Park downtown has never been cleaner
Written By: The Residents of ManorCare, GreenTree
Date: June 10, 2016

Cranberry Place

It's a Burgh Thing
Most men worked in the mill
Why is this such a big deal?
It employed my husband, father, and brother
And many cousins all worked in the mill together
Every town just about had a mill by the river and
An Islay's store with chipped chopped ham for sure
In town, there were several different catholic parishes
The liturgy was in Latin — schools taught parishioners
Money of immigrants went to their own churches instead
Of going to their own homes first — literally "Homestead"
The government gave immigrants land, to settle for 7 years
For those whose countries had no land this brought tears
For joy for opportunities and rights with religious freedom
Maybe even for a lucky soul to reach Hollywood stardom

A Puzzle of the Heart
Every-one of us here has a story
We all experienced some sort of glory
It was the city that made us a bit gritty
The center of our universe was shut down in town
However, Pittsburgh is made up of Pittsburghers
Individuals who've survived and not been kept down
We get up every day ready to work like Steel Workers
Written By: The Residents of Cranberry Place
Date: June 13, 2016

Rochester Manor & Villa

Smoky City Beach
Men and women built LST's
Along the Ohio River in Ambridge
Parents worked hot summer days
Kids built a beach on the river banks
What a feat to swim at Smoky City Beach
A black and white photo in summer's haze
Maybe that's how mother found out about it
And why some boys got a real good licking
You know boys when they enter that phase
Written By: The Residents of Rochester Manor & Villa
Date: June 14, 2016

Independence Court

The Clean Machine
Working on your chainsaw
Your lawn mower and car
To get the grease off
We used Lava soap and mops
We were friends of "Mr. Clean"
Felz Naptha Soap worked and we
Recall using Life Boy for bathing
For the windows just water and vinegar
Or newspaper, baking soda, and water
Clorox Bleach used on lots of things
And we recollect we cannot forget him
The Ajax Knight — cleaning with might

Valley of Decision
The Painter's Row section of the South Side
Existed because of Carnegie Steel's Painter's Mill
Up on the hill was a section called The Chimney Mill
That is part of town that you will no longer find around
Of course, lots of Pittsburgh's history has been torn down
Built up and torn down to the sound of wheels on the rails
Trains with all their cars rocking us, passing by with thrills
Barges, mills, and railroads; it helped if you knew somebody then
Bloomfield is still a working town that is up in the city's hills
It's been known for years that Pittsburgh is "The Smoky City"
That's part of the trade and made a movie "Valley of Decision"
Written By: The Residents of Independence Court, Monroeville
Date: June 15, 2016

Elmcroft

Porch Swing
On a hot summer's day
Our front porch swing in shade
Iron City Beer, Ice tea, lemonade
An ice-cream dairy across the way
Now a busy restaurant open all day
Playing cards, nebbing on neighbors
500 Rummy, Bridge, Go Fish, Old Maid
Sitting on an old-fashioned swing hand-made
Also had one on the back porch in the shade

Porch Ville
Chautauqua Institute in New York
Spent a week with us in Meyersdale, PA
Including all their programming What a deal
It was very exciting for not even going away
Some of us swam in Connoquenessing Creek
Or was up in Cook's Forest for a whole week
We had a fine cottage up in those wooded hills
It was and is nice to stop and take a short break
And at night look up and maybe see shooting stars
Whether we stay right at home or go somewhere far
Written By: The Residents of Elmcroft, Allison Park
Date: June 15, 2016

Ross Hill Retirement

A Day That Sparkles
Christmas in July
A great time for apple pie
Under a clear blue sky
Celebrating the 4th of July
With fireworks and fireflies
All so happy and surprised

Viewing Life in Pittsburgh
Named the 82 Lincoln street car
Her mother took it from downtown far
Up into the East End of the city on Point View
From the street-car, it was up three flights of stairs
Near the top, she'd stop at the sights and stare
Mum worked at Mansmann Department store
She took her shoes off when she got in the door
A friend of mine she volunteered at the U.S.O.
Adjacent from Penn Station it had lots going on
In the game room having fun playing Ping Pong
Pittsburgh had lots of street-cars moving along

Pittsburgh's Golden Year
Looking back, we recall and realize
Downtown we couldn't see sun or sky
But we had much love and civic pride
Smoke's gone and we can't believe our eyes
Written By: The Residents of Ross Hill Retirement
Date: June 16, 2016

Vincentian De Marillac

We Came From Italy to Pittsburgh
When we came to Pittsburgh from Italy
Pittsburghers got around on the trolleys
Abruzzo, Italy to Coraopolis, Pennsylvania
This, of course, across the Atlantic far away
We knew it would be okay though with family
And our church and our friends from Italy
Two children raised without a father in the Army
He was killed at war on foreign land in Germany
Rome, Italy, is different from South Western PA
But in summer, people take to the water similarly
Tourists up in the mountains in winter for skiing
Per me, America and Italy both molto, molto bene'!
Written By: The Residents of Vincentian De Marillac
Date: June 20, 2016

The Pines

Pie in July

If you're gathered around at a picnic table in July
Aside from cheese and fruit for dessert there's pie
Fresh rhubarb! And pumpkin from a can to a surprise
And all the berries growing fresh in the summer wild
Blueberries, blackberries, strawberries, and elderberries
Graham-cracker crust, chocolate pudding, whip cream pie
We love eating pie after dinner while fireflies come alive

Apple pie

Do you like apple pie?
Have you eaten apple pie in July?
One thing for apple pie is a must
Make it or break it—the pie crust!
Granny Apple Smith makes for a good pie
If you ever stop and wonder exactly why
Yes, apple is America's favorite #1 pie...
And not just for eating on the 4th of July!
Written By: The Residents of The Pines, Mt. Lebanon
Date: June 21, 2016

Lighthouse Pointe Village

From the Tower to the Factory to the Farm

Downtown Pittsburgh on the 32nd floor of the Gulf Tower
There was no air conditioning — not in the law department
Women opened windows for fresh air and a view with power
Was a time when the glass factories were alive and thriving
Our family's specialized glass factory keeps on surviving
Though the 32nd floor Gulf Tower windows are sealed now
Red glass, technical specialties, electricity, Pittsburgh aglow
It was seen from our family farm then in the city's Greenfield

Pickled Summer
Fresh pickles that crack when you bite them
My girlfriend and I decided to pickle one weekend
It was nice outside, so my husband painted the car
Inside our house, it smelled like an H.J. Heinz pickle jar!
And in the backyard, it smelled like A PPG paint factory
Oh what I recall of those fond summertime memories
Written By: The Residents of Lighthouse Pointe Village
Date: June 22, 2016

Franciscan Manor

Greetings from Pittsburgh
Romania, Ireland, Germany
Italy, Poland, England, and Japan
Different customs and backgrounds
But it's Pittsburgh we all understand

Nothing Was Thrown Away
We helped Mother grow and can
Fruit and tomatoes. That was the plan
So we could live off of that all winter
Looking back, that plan was a winner
Cherries and peaches from a local farm
Our coal furnace worked like a charm
We had to shovel coal from the chute
Coal, laundry, and shelves of canned fruit
Everything in the cellar indeed purposeful
Nothing thrown away that could be useful
Written By: The Residents of Franciscan Manor
Date: June 22, 2016

Willow Heights

Picturesque City

Here's a picture of downtown back in 1891
I defy you to find me just one blade of grass
Yes, that's right! Nothing but soot, smoke, and ash
Crude as crude can be, yet we love our city's history
Pride in prettiness we find in the grittiness of our city
Slag poured and flowing like lava-like red-stained glass
Written By: The Residents of Willow Heights
Date: June 23, 2016

Willow Lane

Mary Jane

In Pittsburgh, while visiting from Philadelphia
It was Easter Sunday and let me tell ya fella
Wearing my white patent leather Mary Jane shoes
By the end of the day they weren't white anymore
There was soot on the ground up to my relative's door
Written By: The Residents of Willow Lane
Date: June 24, 2016

Beaver Valley Health & Rehab

The 3 Rivers Queen
Pittsburgh's Gateway Clipper set sail back in 1958
Soon the Allegheny, Monongahela, and Ohio saw a fleet
The Gateway Clipper, Party Liner and Good Ship Lollipop
They were all on Pittsburgh's 3 rivers by the mid 1960's
The 50th year anniversary was celebrated back in 2008
Pittsburgh has become a place to see and be seen in 2016
"Gateway to the West" was how Pittsburgh was known...
In 2013, the fleet added its 6th ship, The 3 Rivers Queen

The 3rd Day of Summer
On the 3rd day of summer,
The boys swimming in the river
Taking chances on getting a lickin'
The girls wouldn't take that kinda dance
Whether you were in the water or not
Just you being there made Mom hot
Was easy to get yourself a good lickin'
And much safer to go
Blackberry picking
Written By: The Residents of Beaver Valley Health & Rehab
Date: June 24, 2016

CHAPTER 6

JULY

Wexford House

10 Minutes of July 4th 2016
Soggy hot dogs and buns
Aren't exactly what we call fun
Unless you are Joey "Jaws" Chestnut
He ate 70 hot dogs and soggy buns and won
Nathan's Famous Hot Dog Eating Competition
What a way to celebrate July 4th on Coney Island
Joey Chestnut, apple pie, rides, let the fireworks begin

Summer Days of Pittsburgh
Girls can pitch, hit, and run as well
When we were kids playing ball; if we fell
We got up, shook it off and kept on playing
Didn't run home to our parents, know what I'm saying
Summer barefooted buzz-cut boys and pigtailed little ladies
Written By: The Residents of Wexford House
Date: July 5, 2016

Willow Heights

Heart Shaped Glass
Collecting depression-era-glass
Transcending space and class
What a buy while antiquing in July
Combing stores in PA, WV, and OH for a find
Lots of people are plainly fine with plastic
But my love gave me a heart-shaped glass

1960
It was the bottom of the 9th in October
1960 watching the World Series on TV
I thought the series, the Pirates were over
So I'm in the backyard pulling clothes from the line
Man, suddenly church bells started ringing and
Car horns blowing, people screaming, "Bill Mazeroski!!!"
Everyone in a state of euphoria cheering outside in the streets
"Maz hit a home run! The NY Yankees are beat! Maz made history!"
Written By: The Residents of Willow Heights
Date: July 5, 2016

Marian Manor

Jefferson Beach
Jefferson Beach along the Allegheny out
In Elizabeth, PA is a way from Lincoln -
Place yet all the way we all sure did come
Our 1950's automobiles parked by the shore
Back then the river was mucky with lots of oil
Steel by-product and waste in the water and soil
It was a nice prosperous time back then though
Our mother often would say, "If the smoke stacks

Aren't smoking, the workers aren't working or paid"
Work was hard on us and so on the river, we'd relax

Pot Belly Stove
The train came right along by your house with
Coal for us to pick up with our buckets and lift
And to carry on home after they were full of it
That was in the 1950's until we bought mother
An electric stove in March of that year, which was better
Back when the "Ice Man Delivery" was common
Along with taking a "Chamber-Pot" out the backdoor
To empty out back behind the "Buck-House" out back
Behind our home with a spigot and Clorox to disinfect
Back in that time some mothers still used "Washboards"
Back when we'd hang our laundry on a line to dry in the sky
Written By: The Residents of Marian Manor
Date: July 8, 2016

Eldercrest Nursing Center

Pittsburgh Town and Country History
When all that could survive the Three Rivers were
catfish - bottom dwellers - big mean suckers
North Park had the biggest swimming pool ever
In the USA and second largest in the whole world
The rivers were too polluted to swim in back then
Thanks to the Mellon's, Scaife's and Mayor Lawrence
Pittsburgh has cleaned-up and now bass swim again
The Three Rivers and city has really changed 110 percent

Compared to Pittsburgh
Other cities are too constructed brand new
Pittsburgh has character like you and you
Strolling along downtown streets look-up
Gargoyles and such Romanesque architecture
Our construction has our city's history in view
Like Homestead Waterfront colossal columns
From our city's giant steel mills that have fallen
Written By: The Residents of Eldercrest Nursing Center
Date: July 12, 2016

Ross Hill Retirement

Days Gone By Like Night

Dimlings Candy
On the corner of Liberty and Fifth
A man sold stacks of newspaper
The 82-Lincoln going along long trolley tracks
Its headlight brightly aglow in the morning at 10 a.m.
The streetlights were on like it was after midnight
One didn't need glasses to see only some clean air
Hard to believe it today - The Great Smog of 1938
Nevertheless a picture taken back then says so
That was life in Pittsburgh - Days gone by like night

Sandy Creek Rd

With five kids to raise
We were always out of milk
Finally, the milkman started to deliver
We fetched it from steep house steps
Glass bottles of milk in a metal container
Six quarts of milk twice a week or so
He collected his empty bottles promptly
Always business-like and on the go
Written By: The Residents of Ross Hill Retirement
Date: July 12, 2016

ManorCare

Days of the Party Line

The telephone mounted on the wall
We used to race to pick up and answer the call
These were days of the party line before each home
Had its own separate phone line so you never were alone
Neighbors shared the party line and also their private talk
Which was good for nebby neighbors watching like a hawk

We Weren't Spoiled

Everybody in the city had fans before air conditioning
Had to in summertime - It was hot, so we kept 'em running
All day and all night so we could all sleep well dreaming
Dreaming that the fans didn't jack up the bill increasingly
Yeah these were the days of city life we recollect fondly
Written By: The Residents of ManorCare, Pittsburgh
Date: July 13, 2016

Rochester Manor & Villa

July's Magic Treasures

July comes and goes so quickly
Majestic river valley sunsets bridging
For a magical twilight and dusk with
Lightening bugs rising from green lawns
Carrying the sun's fire when they fly
All the way from night until the dawn
When the sun lights up the blessed sky

School Shopping Days

At the end of the summer in August
We all had shop for school as a must
Back to school shopping $4.50 for
Low cut canvas tennis shoes and
I remember well at the front door
Mom said, "Hey, where's the rest?"
50 cents in change I had and no more
Written By: The Residents of Rochester Manor & Villa
Date: July 14, 2016

ManorCare

We Came A Long Way
Smog is a Pittsburgh word!
Smoke and Fog equals Smog!!
The mills made this word heard
Throughout our three river valleys
Smog and soot in almost every alley

Washboard Hope
We had an automated dishwasher
Yep, my sisters and I did the dishes
And we did them by hand and laundry too
Used a washboard or scrub-board to clean
Washboard playing musicians - so mean -
And that's all part of our Pittsburgh history
Scrub-boards and Lava Soap equal hope to be clean
Written By: The Residents of ManorCare, GreenTree
Date: July 15, 2016

Forbes Center for Rehabilitation and Healthcare

Transitions

Pencil boxes with supplies
Shopping for back to school clothes
Kaufman's where we had a charge
Future turns to present and present to past
July summer days go by us so very fast
Suddenly, we're picnicking on Labor Day
Leaves turning colors under Autumn skies
Kids walking and talking summer vacation
Happy to see all your boy and girl friends again

The Grill on the Hill

The Crawford Grill
Up on the Hill
Everybody was there
Remember seeing George Benson
He had a talent with his guitar
And he could sing and was popular
And he's still a popular figure
Everyone danced to these players
Like The Cadillacs, Earl Garner played
By ear; he played piano, yeah, really and
Billy Eckstein played the Crawford Grill too.
It was a top hot spot, "The Grill on the Hill"
Written By: The Residents of Forbes Center for Rehabilitation &
HealthCare
Date: July 18, 2016

Cumberland Crossing

White Gloves

I took a trolley car to work every day
I worked downtown at Duquesne Light
Spent most lunchtimes at Gimbels workdays
In the morning, I'd put on a pair of white gloves
And at the end of the day going home have another
Spent most of my evenings washing white gloves
It was quite a prosperous time for Pittsburgh
Yes, smoke, soot, and ash so you may have heard
Most men and women could be taken by their word

Honesty

A lot of people ask
Are you doing this for love
For love, it usually doesn't
Matter what is the cost
We even write to show love
And put forth honesty in word
Words of love to guide when lost
Written By: The Residents of Cumberland Crossing
Date: July 19, 2016

Elmcroft

They Don't Know What They're Missing
Kids were allowed to be kids... Now
They all have TV, AC, and games on the phone
Back when we were kids we all shared one phone
And we played hop-scotch and we jumped rope for fun
Right out in front of our houses we sang songs not one
Of us bored at all because we had a ball playing outside
Yep "catch" and "hide and seek" and we "kicked the can" a ton
We were busy being young kids every single day of the week

Clifton Park Steps
We lived in Clifton Park
It's now Chautauqua Street
From 1895 - 1905 there was an Incline
But between then and the bus line in the 40's
We were counting all the stairs we had climbed
There were over 100 some steps that were wooden
Going down was okay, but going up you wanted to die
There's a lot of forgotten history to look up on the North Side
Written By: The Residents of Elmcroft, Allison Park
Date: July 27, 2016

Franciscan Manor

Summer Thoughts
Green rolling hills on each side
Stalks of corn and groups of trees we go by
Driving into blue sky and white puffy clouds
Summer is at its peak for growing season now
Everything is full of vitality and summer beauty
Walking in the heat of afternoon where it's shady
Bright green grass like thick carpeting and it's how
We picture summertime in our minds when February

The Good Old Days
What you don't have, you learn so you don't miss
Ever been out to the "out-house" and hear a hiss
There were creepy critters and crawlers around
And no one had air conditioning not even in town
We walked up and down wooden sets of steps from our
Neighborhoods to other places because that's how it was
We didn't really think about things like being poor so listen
Those days before may have been harder but are well missed
Written By: The Residents of Franciscan Manor
Date: July 27, 2016

Independence Court

The Penny Candy Store

Where everything was a penny
For a nickel, you sure got plenty
Back in those days, good old days
Brother to The Clark Bar was Zagnut
Something else about our good old ways
A dime allowed you to ride the trolley all day
Here is a picture to remember of the "Hucksters"
They had a horse and a cart and sharpened knives
There's nothing better than our good old days and ways

Always Remember the Good Old Days

We always played outside
Summer would easily find
Kids outside playing unless it rained
But some even played out in the rain
As long as no thunder and lightning
Well, we did enjoy our lightening-bugs
Mason-jars filled with fireflies 4th of July
Dark brought the lights turned on at home
Where we were called to come at day's end
Through some tin cans connected by strings
Remember playing "telephone" back when
Remember the good old days, ways, and things
Written By: The Residents of Independence Court, Monroeville
Date: July 28, 2016

CHAPTER 7

AUGUST

Wexford House

Pittsburgh's End of the World 1938
Before smog control and environmental protection agency
Pittsburgh, Pennsylvania was known as "The Smokey City"
White uniforms of nurses and white shirts of men turned
All dirty black with soot that drowned out the morning sun
The "Great Smog of 1938" left the school kids quite frantic
We were frightened not knowing why day looked like night
Dark as midnight at midday with streetlights and headlights on

Sunday, School, and Play Shoes
The first thing mother said when you got home
From a school day was, "Change your shoes – and go
Put your play shoes on!" Some folks called those
Their tennis shoes "tenners" And if they had a big hole,
We would use pieces of cardboard to mend the soles
Written By: The Residents of Wexford House
Date: August 2, 2016

West Hills Health & Rehab

Hot Summertime
Open the windows
Open the doors
It's summer in August
Hot and humid, that's for sure
Before there was air conditioning
We left our house fans running
To stay cool it was a must to do
Written By: The Residents of West Hills Health & Rehab
Date: August 2, 2016

The Pines

Pittsburgh's Got It
You know, in Pittsburgh
Yeah, we might get snow
And hot and humid "dog days
of summer" and an occasional
tornado and seasonal hurricane rains
and ice storms and so far no big
problem with bad mosquitos so
"knock on wood" and give thanks
Grateful for our neck of the woods
Here in Southwestern Pennsylvania
Written By: The Residents of The Pines, Mt. Lebanon
Date: August 3, 2016

Canterbury Place

Backward Chicken Forward Pig
The chicken in the yard scratches backwards
And at the New Year, we all look towards
Good luck with our family's New Year tradition
Pigs root to feed with snouts moving forward
This is our realization and it's an explanation...
When and why we eat pork put forth in a question

Peaceful Summer Day
Dad used to lay on the hammock
His arms folded and radio on his chest
Listening to the baseball game with the
Dog lying underneath him on our porch
Oh, those were the days, all right, yes
I can sure picture that warm summer day
Written By: The Residents of Canterbury Place
August 8, 2016

Cumberland Crossing

The Price of Pittsburgh Soot
White glove clean
At a dirt-cheap price
Cleaning women never
Complained about soot
If there was soot everywhere
That meant ample jobs to put
Women to work every single day
Written By: The Residents of Cumberland Crossing
Date: August 9, 2016

Grace Manor

Our Town
Sharpsburg and Etna
Had mills and factories
Men had main jobs making pipes
Mills and factories created money
The railroad terminal also employed
Back then, you'd pay for a street car
To transfer from Carnegie to Crafton
Some took street cars to the city zoo
All this is Pittsburgh history and is true
Written By: The Residents of Grace Manor
Date: August 9, 2016

ARSP Participants

Activity Directors
Helping those remember (including you)
Saying they wear many hats is true
Fun tricks of the trade and a call for folks to use
Heart, mind, and spirit like a ray on a sunny day

Little Pitchers Have Big Ears
Maybe it was Pig-Latin from siblings
Or language from native tongues talking
We kids picked-up on the tone not totally knowing
Yet we knew it was good stuff for us eavesdropping
Written By: The Residents of ARSP Participants
Date: August 9, 2016

Vincentian De Marillac

City Summers
City people dressed balconies
With flower boxes filled with peonies
We also dressed it up with American flags
Carpeted, furnished terraces of Pittsburgh
Orange canopies and yellow table umbrellas
Ivy topiaries and ivy creeping up brick walls
We grilled meats and had fresh herbs and salads
Tomatoes and lettuce from our terrace city gardens
Written By: The Residents of Vincentian De Marillac
Date: August 12, 2016

Rochester Manor & Villa

A Day at the Movies for 35 Cents
A nickel for a frosted mug of root beer
In New Brighton, Beaver Co. at Isaly's
It stayed a nickel there for about five years
A bottle of 10 ounces cost us a dime and with
A 2 cent deposit when you turned it in empty
15 cents for the show and a nickel worth of candy
At the penny-candy-store where the pretzel sticks
Cost us one penny for three sticks which served as
Our cowboy cigars like the cowboys in the picture shows
Written By: The Residents of Rochester Manor & Villa
Date: August 12, 2016

ManorCare

Old East End Shopping and Dining
Woolworth's and Murphy's Five & Dime
Grant's 5&10 with a nearby Isaly's...
The old east end was a hopping time
On Penn Avenue was Antonino's Restaurant
Bolan's Candies 6018 Penn opened in 1918
Of course, they made candy in East Liberty
But Mr. Bolanis also ran a Greek restaurant
We made 50 cents an hour and lunch cost $1.00

A&P Stores
Before Kroger's and Giant Eagle...
Here comes a good old memory of Pittsburgh
Taking us way back to days of the "A&P" stores
Atlantic and Pacific is what A&P stood for and more
Families had been there than to the movies for sure
Memories of walking with your family with a red wagon
We'd ride in the wagon to the A&P and fill it with groceries
Back then they had same as cash green and yellow stamps
We would use those for all kinds of things from towels to lamps
Written By: The Residents of ManorCare, GreenTree
Date: August 15, 2016

Ross Hill Retirement

Dads of Boomtown U.S.A.
That was a way of life
Pittsburgh was instrumental
During the war, McDowell Manufacturing
They made shells in a factory in Millvale
Folks worked making mortars, and millionaires
were made over and over and some in the mines
Which immigrants worked days before H.J. Heinz
Pittsburgh was the "Smokey City" in a "Boom-time"
People flocked to Pittsburgh from all around to work
Some fathers employed at Crucible Steel in Lawrenceville

The Bambino - The Sultan of Swat
Babe Ruth, the famous N.Y. Yankee
Played a couple of years for the Pittsburgh Pirates
He hit his last home run at Forbes Field at the end of his career
The Bambino - Sultan of Swat played for us as a buccaneer
Del's restaurant in Bloomfield was a known hot spot in town
Guys and gals strolled in and out with maybe even a Pirate around
But that wouldn't be Babe Ruth as Del's didn't open until 1949
By then The Bambino - Sultan of Swat beat-it-on-down-the-line
Written By: The Residents of Ross Hill Retirement
Date: August 16, 2016

Cranberry Place

Part of Pennsylvania Coal Country
Youghiogheny Valley
Has the Youghiogheny River
And is one of the older settlements
People used to work in coal mines there
Now where my family's homestead was
There's tourism and recreation instead
With Ohiopyle and its white water rapids
Trails well supplied with mountain vistas
Rich with plenty of history of Pennsylvania
Written By: The Residents of Cranberry Place
Date: August 16, 2016

Eldercrest Nursing Center

If You're So Inclined
Today there are only two Pittsburgh Inclines
But back in the day there were about seventeen
Several for freight to carry up from the old PL&E
Which is now the location of the Grand Concourse
Fine Pittsburgh dining inside a Historical Landmark
This South Side and Mt. Washington once industrial
Inclines moving heavy freight now quite fashionable
Written By: The Residents of Eldercrest Nursing Center
Date: August 16, 2016

ManorCare

Pittsburgh Vintage

We remember homemade jellies and jam
In mason jars, everything was sure canned
Peppers, tomatoes, peaches, and pears, oh my
String beans, apples, blackberries, strawberries
Luscious blueberries and homemade crust for our pies

Picture Sown In Verse

Reading and listening to poetry
Written when a workshop was inspiring
This came to be when hearing about the city
In fact, she said, "The picture is sown in verse." Of
course, this phrase hit me, spoken so eloquently.
Written By: The Residents of Manorcare, Monroeville
Date: August 18, 2016

Victoria Manor

Bell Telephone
What a difference between the years
of 1930 - 1980 in Pittsburgh, Pennsylvania
Operators ran the telephones in all the city
Would ring your home and ask, "Will you hold?"
They would connect you with the caller if you told
the operator of the line, "Yes, I'll accept the call, dear!"

The Time of the Evening Train Whistle
Nowadays people get to Kennywood Park by car
Back in the day when the town of McDonald was kinda far
Outside from the city of Pittsburgh, Pennsylvania, we took a train
Early in the morning we would start about 7:30 a.m. matter of fact
As the sun was rising in the summer sky and our excitement high too
Hard to contain as we anticipate the wooden rollercoaster ride in June
Written By: The Residents of Victoria Manor
Date: August 19, 2016

ManorCare

A Change of Season in the Breeze
A season long of summer's noon burnt sun
Has covered the canopies with a golden hue
Already leaves are starting to fall one by one
August is wrapping up now for Autumn fun...
Taking long walks in the cool breeze of the day
Things are bright as fall colors such as orange,
yellows, browns, reds, and green show the way
The season changes when fruit ripens on vines
Frost arrives and birds headed south tell its time
Written By: The Residents of ManorCare, Shadyside
Date: August 23, 2016

Franciscan Manor

There's a lot of History Here
From zig zagging Native American Indian trails
To making flights of wooden steps that wouldn't fail
Conquering travel over rivers and their river valleys
Railroads and Inclines taking goods to the old mills
16th Street Bridge topped with horses running a ridge
Some folks paid pennies to cross over rivers on a bridge
And to navigate the rugged Southwestern Pennsylvania terrain
We engineered the Pitt and Squirrel Hill Tunnels and Liberty Tubes
Written By: The Residents of Franciscan Manor
Date: August 23, 2016

Elmcroft

Holding on to Summer
Roses may fade in the fall
When sunflowers stand erect and tall
Under a blue sky and golden sunshine
Hard to say goodbye to precious summertime
Apple pie, Fourth of July fireworks, and fireflies...
Long days filled with beaming summer sunlight
And into extra innings under bright lights at night

Medicine Man
Pittsburgh has a lot of history
Going back to the French and Indian War
Here's one memory seldom shared before
My mother from Spring Hill above North Side
Had an Indian friend who knew how to heal
He would sell my mother different medicines
He must've had herbs and recipes and remedies
I was pretty young but I do recall his name "Red Key"
He was tall with long black hair and was a Shawnee
Written By: The Residents of Elmcroft, Allison Park
Date: August 24, 2016

Beaver Valley Nursing and Rehab

We're All #1
Third place in Senior Olympics
We are all #1 when trying our best
Third place puts our character to a little test
We are all winners and never chose to be less
When we all get together and have help from our friends
Nothing but good wishes and congratulations do we send

Written By: The Residents of Beaver Valley Nursing and Rehab
Date: August 25, 2016

Beaver Eldercare

We Eat Pie Here
Croatians, Italians, Germans, Lebanese,
Irish, Scottish, Jewish, folks all agree
Homemade pie crust is absolutely the best
We've filled pie crust with apples, cherries
pumpkin, cranberry, blueberries and blackberries,
strawberries, rhubarb and our crust passes the test
Written By: The Residents of Beaver Eldercare
Date: August 31, 2016

Willow Lane

School Days
Hearing my name called over the school speaker
From homeroom to the Administration office, my knees got weaker
I could just hear my mother now on how I dishonored her
But as my brain registered it, the principal made me Hall Monitor!
Written By: The Residents of Willow Lane
Date: August 31, 2016

Willow Heights

Bridging Past to Future
The covered bridge was rickety and rackety
Walking with Frick and Frack felt like an eternity
Hooves from horses and cattle going clickety and clapety
October fright nights thinking Headless Horseman at Halloween
Wooden planks replaced by advancements in concrete and steel beams
Written By: The Residents of Willow Heights
Date: August 31, 2016

CHAPTER 8

SEPTEMBER

Rhodes Estates

Roses in Winter
You know what is a bummer?
As days go by, it's the end of summer.
Days are getting shorter & nights longer & colder.
June left way too soon and fall always brings winter.
When only our memories remind us of summer weather,
God made us memory so we can remember roses in winter.

Peripatetic Lifestyle
He wore a pea coat with his collar up
He was a North Atlantic navy man held up
In a port city that was named Reykjavik in Iceland
He was a good looker and wouldn't let ya forget it
Photographers took pictures of him inside of their town
While he was smoking cigarettes, drinking, hanging around
Written By: The Residents of Rhodes Estates
Date: September 1, 2016

Cumberland Crossing

Canning the Harvest
Labor Day takes
Summer away. It
Doesn't take way our fun though,
Because in fall...
We have a ball.
Fall is beautiful.
And magical in the
Harvest time where
It is also practical,
As harvest is preserved
Canning is economical.
Fresh taste is superior!
Written By: The Residents of Cumberland Crossing
Date: September 2, 2016

Grace Manor

Everyday Memories
A ringer-washer in the basement
Hanging a line to dry clothes in the yard
A rot iron bathtub filled with lye & lots of lard
The past when we folks made homemade soap
With memories of cookies made with a little lard
Baked in love, raisins, oatmeal and heaven sent
These kinda memories are the ones that harvest hope
Written By: The Residents of Grace Manor
Date: September 2, 2016

West Hills Health & Rehab

Strawberry Pie
Strawberries in the garden
We used to pick them and
Sometimes we'd make crust
With a little touch of lard in it
Trick of the trade for fluffy crust
So it doesn't taste like baked sand
The crust is as important furthermore
As the fresh strawberries of the garden

Daddy
He used a hatchet
He was a handy man
His arms, chest, and back
Were all very strong like an Ox
He cut steps out of the earth;
Steps we used to climb the hills
And the pride of doing was his pay
Written By: The Residents of West Hills Health & Rehab
Date: September 6, 2016

Antonia Hall

Pittsburgh Neighbors

Out east across the state from Pittsburgh
There were cement and silk mills we've heard
From those who have transplanted to Pittsburgh
Some mothers worked as silk weavers and others
Men worked as managers in cement mills together
Like in South Western PA or out near Philadelphia
Our families and our kin-folk are community oriented

Bring a Ring

128 steps by the Uniondale Cemetery
We used to climb those to go to high school
Lugging heavy books, our knees would go weak
Some of us took street cars to town and school
Many fathers worked in mills at the age of twenty
3 shifts, 18 hrs, but around your girl no time to doze
Within those 6 free hours better be ready to propose
Written By: The Residents of Antonia Hall
Date: September 7, 2016

Marian Hall

Pie Crust
We'd rather have
If given a fair chance
Homemade pie crust
With a little lard for fluff
Puffy, flaky homemade
Not the store-bought
Homemade is the best
Hot apple pies in July &
Pumpkin for Thanksgiving

Pig Hill
Pig Hill going from East Ohio Street
Up top on Troy Hill with the livestock
From over across the river in the Strip
Driving live stock on the 16th St Bridge;
Wooden it was and farms up in the hills
Pigs were killed in slaughter houses to eat
Late 1800's & early 1900's work week to week
Written By: The Residents of Marian Hall
Date: September 7, 2016

Franciscan Manor

The Greenery of Pittsburgh
Unlike the Pittsburghers of the past
We have become environmentally aware
We have recycling of materials in marked bins
Newspaper, plastic, glass, aluminum, and yes tin
Franciscan Manor is part of the new Pittsburgh...
On the internet you can even take a Google tour

That's right; a virtual reality tour here to learn more
Written By: The Residents of Franciscan Manor
Date: September 9, 2016

Paramount Senior Living

Whole Foods Fantasy
In 1906, the H.J. Heinz House
The original from Sharpsburg
Hundreds gathered shoulder to shoulder
Standing to see the spectacle on the river
Home of Heinz floated down the Allegheny City
Now the North Side but still the site of H.J. Heinz
Women workers in clean uniforms looked pretty
H.J.Heinz as an employer was a real do-gooder
The Heinz dream for family, company, & city realized
Written By: Paramount Senior Living
Date: September 13, 2016

Rochester Manor & Villa

Fall Colors Bring Steeler Fever
Driving through New Sewickley Township
Cornstalks turning yellow and brown
It is now that time of the year...
We look around and see fall everywhere
The grass adds a golden hue to the ground
Look at those orange pumpkins so round
Round in the patches out on the old farm
The old farm on the outskirts of our town
On the road with Steeler flags hanging down
Written By: The Residents of Rochester Manor & Villa
Date: September 14, 2016

Elmcroft

September Day in Pittsburgh
Taking a walk outside this time of year
September brings something different in the air
We enjoy these bright sunny cool crisp mornings
Flowers that stand out full of color and in bloom
Walking passed them brings scents of perfume
Apples on branches ripened and falling off trees
As the sun climbs the sky we enjoy a warm breeze
Written By: The Residents of Elmcroft, Allison Park
Date: September 14, 2016

Ross Hill Retirement

My Hometown

A quite little town not far from the hustle and bustle of the big city.
A town where people live, work, & pray Together
A town of ethnic backgrounds, German, Croatian, and English
A town where love abounds. With your neighbor the doors were never locked
A town where growing up you learn respect, love & kindness toward others.
A town where men worked hard in the mills.
A town I'm proud to call my home town
Millville.
Written By: Frank Capan at Ross Hill Retirement
Date: September 20, 2016

That's Pittsburgh!

In all of these little river towns
All these towns, boroughs & municipalities
All nestled in the hills and along the bluffs
There is something at Steeler parties to be found
Aside from Iron City Beer, the smell of grilled kielbasa.
Kielbasa and beer, chips & dips until all of us are stuffed
Steeler game day we all bleed black & gold, whatever nationality
Written By: The Residents of Ross Hill Retirement
Date: September 20, 2016

Beaver Valley Health & Rehabilitation Center

Fall Family and Friends
Today is the first day of fall
Summer is officially over for now
In Pymatuning, we saw a woman float her head
Along the gentle wave of the lake while on vacation
Corn is now turning brown, and leaves cover the ground
All the flowers of spring and summer in winter go dead
The kids are back in school; pumpkin seeds are roasting
In ovens across the nation getting ready to bake great pies
Written By: The Residents of Beaver Valley Health & Rehabilitation Center
Date: September 22, 2016

Willow Heights

The Indian Mound
The mound is all but leveled now
From the Ohio River banks to town limits
For men, women, & children it is no gimmick
This mound in the hills was sacred burial ground
Folks were afraid to work there because of spirits
Bones, skulls & arrowheads were found all around the
Ancient Indian burial ground we call "The Indian Mound"
Written By: The Residents of Willow Heights
Date: September 22, 2016

Cranberry Place

Shoulders of the Past
On a big white Arabian horse
We'd set off on a unknown course
He was Snow White and nicknamed "Snow King"
Going by, folks in the neighborhood all knew him
They'd all sing "There goes the girl on her Snow King"
With an interest of historical places for a personal diary
Turned into written essays which brought praise for me
We share a common desire to live and record our history

We Matter
A lot of we girls kept a diary
We didn't dare show it to anyone
Especially those who would find it funny
We would write in it almost every single day
We would write about daily accounts & encounters
A lot of feeling went into writing our diary the way
We would feel & see things differently or the same
Sometimes kept in an old shoe box as we grew older
Sometimes thrown out or burned as winter got colder
Written By: The Residents of Cranberry Place
Date: September 23, 2016

Forbes Center for Rehabilitation and Healthcare

Westinghouse Glory Days Football
On Highland Avenue
All along in a row
SunDrug Pharmacy, Murphy's,
Woolworth, Grant's in the East End
Regent Sq., Liberty, Sheridan, Enright
These were al theaters in the East End
The library was on Finland Avenue and
Original Hotdog Stand with lots to chew
We were there after football games with you
Coach gave we fans lots to cheer about

Friday Nights
Walking home from the library with friends
Good times after football games in the East End
What a treat to stop at the Original Hotdog Stand
With a fountain Coca-Cola and fries in our hands
A foot long hotdog + only a nickel for a jukebox song
We cherish our friends and for these times we long
Written By: The Residents of Forbes Center for Rehabilitation and Healthcare
Date: September 26, 2016

Sweetbriar Place

Kiss Me on the Lips
The colors of the garden will not fade
Corns maybe brown and sunflowers droop
Pink, red, and yellow roses grown in loops
Trellises against the sky blue sky fall days
Long as you kiss me on the lips before I die
The color of May gardens won't fade by winter
I'll be warm while resting and never ever shiver
Written By: The Residents of Sweetbriar Place
Date: September 27, 2016

Mt. Nazareth Commons

Farmer's Market Special
Concord grape vineyards in Connellsville
We made grape jelly to giveaway and keep
Lots of sugar for strawberry, blueberry, and blackberry jelly
Some of us around the city canned jars of Piccalilli
Sweet and sour and red cabbage and homemade sauerkraut
Cucumbers harvested to make jar bread and butter pickles
Nowadays, if you want homemade you gotta go up to Perrysville
Written By: The Residents of Nazareth Commons
Date: September 28, 2016

Vincentian De Marillac

Shopping Down in the Strip
From Polish Hill on Herron
And 22nd Street on Penn
We walked to the Strip District
To people watch, mingle & shop
Sometimes we'd have coffee & tea
Before we'd buy chickens from Dick's
We carried it home & mom dressed it
We kids knew how chickens were fixed

We Call That City Chicken
You're from the city of Pittsburgh
When you eat barbecued pork on a stick
Yet you call it city-chicken & lick your lips
And finger too because it's so good...
It's pork, not chicken, but what-are-you-gonna-do
Written By: The Residents of Vincentian De Marillac
Date: September 29, 2016

Willow Lane

Sweet to Eat
Jenny Lee Bakery
Island Avenue in McKees Rocks
Shame it's not in town anymore
Shame it burned down to the ground
Shame we can't enter its doors anymore
It opened in 1938 & closed too early in 2008
Some of us 1st walked in there at the age of 8

Our Generation
The neighborhoods were close knit
For penny candy, we were at the A&P to shop
For a nickel, we got a lot and thought we were it
Some of us grew & got custodian jobs with a mop.
While others studied books at the University of Pitt
Written By: The Residents of Willow Lane
Date: September 30, 2016

Northview Estates

The Poetry of You
Before the Lincoln High School was built
The Hotel Oliver of 1890 was a nice resort
Built to attract a clientele loaded-to-the-hilt
In fact, Ellwood City got a mill from U.S. Steel
At 5th & Crescent became the Lawrence Hotel
Walking to school and work on Lawrence Avenue
Summer, fall, winter & spring, the town bell rings

Halloween Memories
What's really something great?
We at Northview Estates!
We residents!
With childhood memories
Of Halloween "trick or treat"
Dressing up as Presidents
And famous movie stars
With long sequin dresses
Collecting lots & lots of candies
Back then everything was dandy!
Written By: The Residents of Northview Estates
Date: September 30, 2016

CHAPTER 9

OCTOBER

ManorCare

The Huckster
Like a little A&P store on wheels
The Huckster who came around knew the deal
He'd always give you a better price than the store
We'd wait the days until the Huckster man came around
He'd have most things needed but if you needed any more
He'd write it down with his pencil & pad for a special order
Bring him newspapers bundled in a stack & get money back
With the Huckster man, he'd save you money + make you money
Not only in Pittsburgh neighborhoods, the Huckster was everywhere

A Pie in the Eye
If you can't make a good crust, you see,
Then you can't make a pie for me!
If we felt like good homemade berry pie
We'd wait until the day the Huckster arrived
He'd sing the names of the berries fresh that day
He had a scale to weigh how much you had to pay
Eating hot piping homemade pie is the only way
"This homemade pie crust is to die for!" they all say
Written By: The Residents of ManorCare, GreenTree
Date: October 3, 2016

West Hills Health & Rehab

The Bonfire
At the bonfire for the pep-rally
The fire was so bright it really
Lit up the high school grounds where
We were cheering on the football team
We had hot chocolate with marshmallows & cream
We listened to the cheerleaders scream
"Go Bananas! B-A-N-A-N-A-S! Go Bananas!
B-A-N-A-N-A-S! Go Bananas! B-A-N-A-N-A-S! Go Bananas!"
What a ball we had those fall days and nights of school
"School days, school days-good old fashioned rule days!"

We Did Quite a Job
I lived in the country
But I worked inside the city
As a clerk at G.C. Murphy
My husband, dad & brother drove
I didn't drive but I sold things like
Hats, scarves, socks, gloves, & candy
Everyone loved me and why not you see
Written By: The Residents of West Hills Health & Rehab
Date: October 4, 2016

Antonia Hall

Everyone Is an Original
If we were to create a tapestry
All together to display in Antonia Hall
We'd include silk and cement mills so gritty
Steps of city neighborhoods by big cemeteries
Community places of worship of different ethnicities
Gathered at tables bowing our heads ever so humbly

Pittsburgh Potpourri
We walk down the block
We are hit by our senses
The pungency of 3 rivers
Manufacturing...
The essence of industry
Bridges and buildings
Span the landscape of our city
Pockets of ethnic neighborhoods
Simmer terrifically in cast iron pots
Written By: The Residents of Antonia Hall
Date: October 5, 2016

Marian Hall

In Your Easter Bonnet
People stood on the sidewalks
Singing and cheering and staring
At the Sunday-best this day...
Of those in the Easter parade
This was a delightful celebration
Each year every Easter Sunday

The Worst Flood in Pittsburgh's History
All through the streets there were muddy waters
Even after most of the flood from the rivers receded
It was super dangerous for families & sons & daughters
Lots of help for clean-up and good-will was needed
Many of our homes were complete and utter wrecks
Some folks' homes were off so bad they gave up and left
Written By: The Residents of Marian Hall
Date: October 5, 2016

Rhodes Estates

Rum & Coke

Listening to music and drinking at the bar
We watch and order rum & coke while he's on guitar
He sings a song about a night that went a little too far
More than two rum & cokes he had drank at the bar
When we woke up, it felt like it had been weeks of sleep
Memory dancing with Captain Morgan who's light on his feet!
Written By: The Residents of Rhodes Estates
Date: October 6, 2016

Grace Manor

Toothbrush?

Trick or Treat
Smell my feet
Give me something good to eat!
Children think it's kinda neat
Like wearing Jack-O-Lanterns for shoes
Have you heard the news?
Trick or Treat someone has to lose
The ghost said, "Boo!"
The lady said, "How are you?"
"Would you like to bob-for-apples too?"
The dentist gave us toothpaste & a brush
We all ran from his house in quite a rush!
Written By: The Residents of Grace Manor
Date: October 6, 2016

Elmcroft

Pittsburgh Then & Now

Riding the incline and looking at a beautiful city
Tall buildings, many bridges and now it is so pretty
The 3 rivers sparkle with sunshine instead of dust
And smoke creating such smog no-one could see
We still pay tribute through artwork to all the rust
Take a trip to our museums to see what we mean
The H.J. Heinz, Frick, Andy Warhol, and Carnegie
Written By: The Residents of Elmcroft, Chippewa
Date: October 7, 2016

Rochester Manor & Villa

It Ain't Over Until It's Over

Confetti fell from tall buildings
Offices closed down and so did 5th Avenue
The city was jubilant with this historic victory
Pittsburgh won the World Series and made history
Ending the series with a huge home run from Mazeroski
And those of us who were babes 56 years ago in 1960
We may have slept through it at the time but it has created
A lasting impression in the public consciousness of our fair city
With a first class ticket and priceless memory only costing $7.50
Written By: The Residents of Rochester Manor & Villa
Date: October 13, 2016

Forbes Center for Rehabilitation and Healthcare

City Huckster Man

Up and down and all along the streets of the city
Were people, trolleys, autos & horse drawn carts
The Huckster Man had himself a real good heart
With fair prices for produce and stuff from the start
Huckster Man was a favorite of our block on Friday
The day when our neighborhood fell in his territory
He had his sample we'd call "the plug" and get to eat
All of those dark watermelon triangles so tasty sweet

A Day to Remember

Walking the steps of Penn with the dog
Our Doberman pincher God knows I so love
We make good memories of fall with leaves now gold
We stop in our tracks at the crunching sound learned young
Thoughts of our beloved dog and cat friends now take hold
We remember those who came here before us to reach
Us in ways we won't ever forget like light on a darkened beach
Written By: The Residents of Forbes Center for Rehabilitation and
Healthcare
Date: October 13, 2016

Eldercrest Nursing Center

Trick or Treat
Trick or Treat
Smell my feet
Give me something good to eat!
I'm dressed as Little-Bo-Peep
But I'm not counting sheep
It's Halloween
If you have a sheet
Or have a broom
You got yourself a costume!
And you can go collect candy
Or play a trick feeling randy!
Written By: The Residents of Eldercrest Nursing Center
Date: October 18, 2016

Cranberry Place

Trick or Treat on Halloween
In the 1920's before Interstate 79
And a time when there was only Rt. 19
All kinds of kids did dress up for Halloween
Back when around here was all farm land
Pumpkins matured in pumpkin patches in time
To make fabulous and frightening Jack-O-Lanterns
Potato & flour sacks used for wonderful costumes
All you needed was a sheet, a hat, and a broom
And you can be a witch, a ghost, scarecrow, or zombie
Written By: The Residents of Cranberry Place
Date: October 21, 2016

Ross Hill Retirement

What a Friend Is

A true friend is someone -who does for you without asking for payment
A friend is someone- you can call anytime for help
A friend is someone- who is a sounding board
A friend is someone- who asks for nothing
A friend is someone- you never forget
A friend is life long
Can I be your friend?

What Is Love

Love is the beginning of a beautiful
& lasting relationship
Love is sharing yourself with another
Love is unconditional
Love is never forgetting the one you lost
Love is always in your heart -
you have to find it
Love sometimes gives you -
another chance at love
Love for a second time -
is a blessing from above
Written By: Frank Capan, RossHill Retirement
Date: October 21, 2016

Elmcroft

I'll Be You - You Be Me
With the porch light on
The game is now on
Trick or treat...
Sometimes we'd make
Taffy apples on sticks
Lots of dressed up kids
Baseball players...
All kinds of clowns around
Ghosts who go "BOO!"
With witches all over town
Trick or treat...
A pillow case is handy
For collecting your candy

The Corner Store
Children did not complain
Carrying grocery bags from the A&P
We had to do it even in the rain
Plus some of us up in the hills
Had to go up & down sets of big steps
We had to hurry it up and run before
The bottom of the bag got too wet
Crashing to the sidewalk all our eggs
Written By: The Residents of Elmcroft, Allison Park
Date: October 21, 2016

Franciscan Manor

My Personal Diary Pages
Inside the doors of a friary
It's kept nice inside of priories
It's also something that's very private
Like writings on the pages of our diaries
Something we don't want to share
We used to write a lot about our feelings
Space we could bounce ideas off the ceiling
We expressed things we didn't want others to see
And that is why our diaries were under lock and key
Special moments recorded with loved ones & friends
Inside our diaries on those pages, our memory never ends

Lovely Thoughts of Joanie My Dolly
My mother had a China Doll
She was the size of a baby
She had such a beautiful face
Above her raised velvet collar
Cherub round with rosy cheeks
I felt like she was one of my own
As I pushed her a long in the carriage
I had a glimpse of me in my marriage
I shared this thought with my sister
About the boy I wanted for my mister
Written By: The Residents of Franciscan Manor
Date: October 24, 2016

Mt. Nazareth Commons

Stara
"Rags! Ole iron!"
The man with the horse & carriage
Before they came around in trucks
The Huckster, he sharpened our knives
We had an umbrella man who came by too
An extra ear of corn or 2 for some moonshine
The old Slovak man who sold us all produce
The homemade moonshine made him feel fine

Little Rascals
Playing around apple trees in the fall
We sometimes used an apple for a ball
We played catch with whatever worked
Apples that were sour & some sweet or tart
We played with our imaginations and a lot of heart
When we did have a real store-bought actual ball
We used to use black electrical tape to keep it together
We used rocks, cans, rags, and cardboard for our bases
With the World Series in our minds, we were called to start
Written By: The Residents of Mt. Nazareth Commons
Date: October 26, 2016

Beaver Valley Health & Rehabilitation Center

Halloween Mystery
The night of Halloween
Opening the door what might we see?
On the sidewalks what might we find?
Look over there! Here comes Frankenstein!!!
And that guy looks like he works in the coal mine.
Floating in the air is "Casper- The Friendly Ghost"...
A witch at the party to be your hostess with the most
At Beaver Valley Health & Rehab Center what a fright
All at our spooky haunted-house on trick or treat night!
Written By: The Residents of Beaver Valley Health & Rehab Center
Date: October 27, 2016

Willow Heights

It's Halloween in Pittsburgh
It's Halloween and what do you see?
Goblins, witches, ghosts, a guy from the Navy
Pumpkins carved displaying witches' hats & cats
Pumpkins with painted faces & glued on googly eyes
The smell of fall all around under spooky October skies
Written By: The Residents of Willow Heights
Date: October 27, 2016

CHAPTER 10

NOVEMBER

West Hills Health & Rehab

Our Dream House
In Amherst out on the farm
Out in the country known as Woodlands
Where fruit trees grew in orchards
Berry patches, gardens, and flooded creeks
The house is still standing by the trees
Canning and churning butter. But as for milking,
Those cows were moody and it's like an art
It's like a science to get "old Bessie" a flowing
Written By: The Residents of West Hills Health & Rehab
Date: November 1, 2016

Rhodes Estates

Hula Doll
Our Navy man
He was lean and tan
He had been stationed in Hawaii
I was standing by the record machine
Hoping that he would take notice of me
I was playing Let It Rock by Chuck Berry
And I had just turned the age of nineteen
Later on when we began to go out on dates
I knew it might be something some call fate
He serenaded me with a song on his ukulele
In Hula dancing, each movement has meaning

Written By: The Residents of Rhodes Estates
Date: November 3, 2016

Grace Manor

Welcome Home
Red and yellow, green and brown
Fall leaves falling on the ground
How many of us travel on the road
To grandmother's house we go
At the table pumpkin pie a la mode
That's dessert plus pecan pie we hope
Butterball the premium bird is the word
It even has a turkey crisis hotline to call
If it's a dinner going bad you need solved
#1 make sure your bird is thawed through
Stuffing, cranberries and mashed potatoes too
Around our table it's a pleasure having you
Written By: The Residents of Grace Manor
Date: November 3, 2016

Harbor Senior Living

Providing for the War Effort

Jams, Jellies, and preserves
Are a great way to enjoy fruit
Strawberries fall into that suit
In the days of wartime WWII
We even saved cooking grease
Boy-scouts learned how to lead
Women helped out by canning
Canning for home & the war effort
Matriarchs taught daughters by hand
With the old recipes easy to understand
If you didn't go to war you helped at home
Organized support so soldiers didn't feel alone
Some took the role as Air Raid Wardens while
Soldiers fought for freedom chilled to the bone

Where We Came From

Inside the licorice factory
A long time ago we worked there
Some of us worked on heavy machinery
Some of us women wore nets on our hair
At lunchtime we all went for Coca-Colas
Come on ladies & gentlemen we have a show
Where dirty factory workers get cleaned- up
With Lava Soap cleaning fresh like Irish spring
Which made us whistle to the maidens of Ireland
Everybody in the world saw us as being so happy
Sharing where we came from in our happy stories
Individually and as we who make families & cities
Written By: The Residents of Harbor Senior Living
Date: November 7, 2016

Marian Hall

The Holidays
It will be 2017
This New Year's Day
There has been lots we've seen
And a lot we have enjoyed tasting
The perfection of a crispy turkey skin
On Thanksgiving Day "the Holidays" begin
Roasting turkey and baking ham and pies
At Christmas time what a joy it is to be alive
Written By: The Residents of Marian Hall
Date: November 9, 2016

Antonia Hall

We're Thankful for You
We do remember
How we celebrate in November
Always being grateful at Thanksgiving
Let us view now where we are living
Locations may change and sometimes faces
But at the table we all pray for God's grace
We're all people too and we're thankful for you
Written By: The Residents of Antonia Hall
Date: November 9, 2016

Rochester Manor & Villa

The American Soldier's Way

When you were a kid
You opened the lid
To a can of toy soldiers
Green were the color of Army men
We could play army almost anywhere
Our toy soldiers were not taught fear
Our toy soldiers battled night and day
To protect and serve The American Way
Written By: The Residents of Rochester Manor & Villa
Date: November 10, 2016
*Written in honor of Veteran's Day

Willow Heights

For a Happy Thanksgiving Day

Who are you going to call?!
Butterball! The premium bird
They have the answers
...Haven't you heard?!
Thaw out your bird
How many days in the refrigerator?
Do not leave to thaw on the counter!
You need to get up at dawn
This information you can bank-on!
Those with trouble seeing are lucky
If given a talking thermometer
To help gauge the barometer
Of a gorgeous turkey dinner being tasty
Which equals a Happy Thanksgiving Day!
Written By: The Residents of Willow Heights
Date: November 10, 2016

Cranberry Place

Thanksgiving Blessings
It smells good in here
The aroma from the turkey
Baked homemade bread and pumpkin pie
Tasting how all the ingredients come alive
Especially dressing cooked inside the cavity
Sitting at the table by the warmth of the fire
The hall is filled with joyous cheer & laughter
Perfect is the caramelized pecan pie on a dish
Kids decide who'll pull the turkey bone for a wish
When we leave, it's with bitter-sweet hugs and goodbye
"Thanks for everything!" you hear us say, driving away
So grateful for the holidays and every day in between
For after all, this is what Thanksgiving really means
Written By: The Residents of Cranberry Place
Date: November 18, 2016

Cumberland Crossing

Thanksgiving Feast
We awaken to the smell of turkey
And can tell stuffing must be inside that bird
Because of the aroma of sage & rosemary
It fills the hallways and noses of us all...
It's hard for us to wait when we pull out to baste
The golden skin looks perfect to taste
Standing there ready to touch it & let the feast begin
But we hear the voice of Grandma saying, "It'll be a sin."
Written By: The Residents of Cumberland Crossing
Date: November 28, 2016

Beaver Valley Health and Rehab

Thanksgiving Day in Beaver County
The night before Thanksgiving Day
America stirs with such sweet anticipation
"Happy Thanksgiving Day!" we awaken in the morn
The greeting is as clear as a big beautiful brass horn
We can smell turkey cooking and pumpkin pies baking
We touch all the welcoming hands held out for shaking
The cinnamon used in the candied yams is to our tasting
With friends that are near & dear to us we all are celebrating
Written By: The Residents of Beaver Valley Health and Rehab
Date: November 28, 2016

Franciscan Manor

A Thanksgiving Day Touchdown
What a sight it is, cooking and baking in the kitchen
We hear a song from the Macy's Thanksgiving Day parade
That is describing the carriage a couple were hitched-in
The aroma of Turkey fills the air from the oven in our home
Greeting family with cheer and a smile drawing near touching them
After we've sat and all have had their fill partaking in our giant feast
At the table with desert plates we have pumpkin pie with some coffee
What are you thankful for this year? Come on please tell us all...
We're thankful for everything and everyone and the tastes of fall
And we fans of the Steelers hope for luck today running the football
Written By: The Residents of Franciscan Manor
Date: November 29, 2016

CHAPTER 11

DECEMBER

Grace Manor

Christmas Wishes and Kisses
Sharing is a selfless act of caring
The way the tree is decorated together as we
Candles in the windows, garland and lights on the tree
Sparkling ornaments shining like bright Christmas stars
Listening to tales of Christmas past describing who we are
Three Wise Men, The Kings, The Holy Family in Bethlehem
Behold the baby Jesus with gifts of gold, frankincense & myrrh
Setting up the manger scene we kiss baby Jesus on the forehead
We smell cookies baking for Jolly Old St. Nick, Santa dressed in red
We eat turkey, sweet potatoes, ham, pumpkin & apple pie & candy kisses
Under the mistletoe with you where our kisses fulfill our Christmas wishes
Written By: The Residents of Grace Manor
Date: December 1, 2016

Rhodes Estates

Christmas Senses
Up in the hills it's snowing
See the snow out on the farm
Hear us sing Deck the Halls around
Town caroling in the streets arm & arm
Smell our kettle corn strung with the lights
All around our 12- foot pine looking so fine
Tastes of eggnog & cookies are such delight
Feeling full of good Christmas cheer all night

Off to the Moon
Superman. Wonder woman.
The Green Lantern and the Flash
Pop culture, Sci-Fi super heroes
We read about them in comic books
And listened on the radio of the past
Imaginations running wild- no doubt
On color TV we watched Steve Austin
He's The Bionic Six- Million-Dollar Man
In 1975, The Bionic Woman came alive
Spent summers watching Jaime Sommers
In the 80's, it was Mr. T. in the A-Team van.
Written By: The Residents of Rhodes Estate
Date: December 1, 2016

Marian Hall

Merry Christmas
In church on Christmas Day
We participate and celebrate this way
Hearing the children's choir sing carols
We go home to a house filled with good smells
A fresh cut pine tree and cookies being baked
We've been waiting to taste since we awaked
An after dinner stroll gazing at Dept. store windows
We meet & greet family under the Kaufmann's clock
"Merry Christmas" we say and our cheer never stops
Written By: The Residents of Marian Hall
Date: December 6, 2016

West Hills Health & Rehab

Trimming the Trees

It looks a lot like Christmas at West Hills today
Pretty colored lights, ornaments, and baby Jesus in the hay
Taste the cookies cut in shapes of snowmen, stars, and pine trees
They are decorated with icing and jimmies for Christmas Day
Hot chocolate fills our nostrils along with the smell of Christmas Tree
Hear us sing "Jingle bells, jingle bells, jingle all the way. -Oh What fun!"
We greet everyone with good Christmas cheer, kisses, and hugs
Written By: The Residents of West Hills Health & Rehab
Date: December 6, 2016

Antonia Hall

The Star That Leads Us to Jesus Christ

We know when it's the Christmas season
And it's Baby Jesus that's our true reason
Three Wise Men and barnyard animals around
In the stable where Christ our savior was born
Shepherds in the fields heard the angel's horn
We celebrate mass and enjoy eggnog & cookies
The smell of fresh-cut pine fills the square in town
Under the mistletoe we share our hugs and kisses
We go to bed joyfully dreaming of Christmas wishes
Written By: The Residents of Antonia Hall
Date: December 7, 2016

Ross Hill Retirement

A Jingle Bell Christmas
Eating freshly baked cookies
Trimming the Christmas Tree
We smell the freshly cut pine
Kids to see Santa waiting in line
Rocking around town singing jingles
Hugging our friends it's time to mingle
It's the reason good for the joyful season

Sights and Sounds of Christmas
The Lawrence Welk Show, Andy Williams, Bop Hope
Bing Crosby, Perry Como, Tony Bennett, Dolly Patton
Santa Claus was always the star of these Christmas shows
Watching on the TV and hearing the audience all singing along
Most show sets included troops who had their families all around
Back then we all dressed up for midnight mass on Christmas Eve
Recalling red berries of the holly and sappy pine for the wreaths
Visiting family from Christmas Eve to New Year's Day all that week
Entertained by the train chugging along all around the Christmas tree
Written By: The Residents of Ross Hill Retirement
Date: December 13, 2016

Rochester Manor and Villa

Christmas Magic
Waking up Christmas morning to a blanket of snow
Presents under the tree the ones for me I'll show
Listening to Christmas carols celebrating around the tree
With my family there are plenty of hugs and kisses for me
Smells of 7 Fishes, turkey, and stuffing, plus homemade pierogi
We smell fresh pine and a fire in the fireplace lit up and aglow
Pumpkin, apple & pecan pies, figs, and candy canes taste so good
Great and yummy for our tummy we take a break to say "oh my"
Stockings hung up in a row, mistletoe, and snowflakes in the sky
Written By: The Residents of Rochester Manor and Villa
Date: December 14, 2016

Northview Estates

A Senior Christmas Poem
The countdown for Christmas is on...
Only 9 days left until the big day on the 25th
Maybe we'll be having a white Christmas day
We know we'll be caroling, singing Christmas songs like
"Jingle Bells," "Silent Night," "Santa Claus is Coming to Town,"
"Sleigh Ride," "Rudolph," and "We Wish You A Merry Christmas
And a Happy New Year"and tasting Christmas cheer all year long
Celebrating the birth of baby Jesus Christ, the light of the world
Just like the manger scene under the decorated Christmas tree
This is what it is for me and for we who love the Christmas season
Written By: The Residents of Northview Estates
Date: December 16, 2016

Beaver Valley Health and Rehab Center

Christmas Ingredients
The Christmas Tree decorated with lights
Presents and ornaments make a morning so bright
We hear the sounds of a puppy dog to our delight
Christmas carol music and sleigh bells ringing
We smell hot cocoa and cookies baking in the oven
Warm gooey chocolate peanut butter balls taste heavenly
With hugs & kisses, we celebrate Christmas day magnificently
Written By: The Residents of Beaver Valley Health and Rehab Center
Date: December 22, 2016

Willow Heights

Christmas Time Again
People scurrying all about town
Some with pine trees and presents to wrap
Bells, ringing Christmas caroling arm & arm
From city sidewalks to sleighing out on the farm
Smell the fresh cut pine we haul home with its sticky sap
Home by the fire with hot chocolate before the mall to see Santa
The kids all lined-up to sit on Santa's lap for their Christmas wish
Santa says, "Were you naughty or nice? Let me check my list twice!"
Written By: The Residents of Willow Heights
Date: December 22, 2016

CHAPTER 12

TESTIMONIALS

Testimonials

John,

I wanted to take a minute to thank you. My Grandmother, Ann, was a resident for 3 years at Franciscan Manor. I realize you didn't know her personally, but she listened to your readings. You have a great way, and it's pretty special. Thank you so much for being a part of her 98-year journey and for making her last days brighter. You do great work for a noble cause and I'm glad to know you.

Thanks again and God Bless.

Gary Young

▲ ▲ ▲

I am writing this letter in regards to the poetry sessions we have once a month. I was never interested in poetry, but my first time with John seemed to spark my interest.

John is an inspiration when we get together. We pick a subject, we provide comments or a line and all of a sudden we have a poem.

I must say, more people should try it and find out for themselves how it can relax and start you thinking about people, places and things. You never would have thought you could come up with a poem. It is surprising how fast an hour goes by and you feel good afterwards. I look forward to it each month. I have written three poems!

Frank Capan

Testimonials

Our poetry workshops have become an important part of our community. The residents love to reminisce about the past, socialize, and learn new things about their friends here at the Rochester Manor and Villa. It is very fulfilling and exciting for our residents to see their memories come to life in poetry form.

John's excitement and passion about poetry is infectious and our residents look forward to his visit and the next topic of discussion.

One of our residents was so inspired by the poetry class that he has started writing his own poems that are printed in our monthly newsletter! Carl had this to say about the class: "I love John's poetry class because he gives me different view about Pittsburgh and he encourages us to be creative and think about the past."
Rochester Manor and Villa

Made in the USA
Columbia, SC
21 September 2021